with all good wishes

Grace, 07 March
2018

6 Report

Religion in Public Life:
Levelling the Ground

Grace Davie

Foreword by Peter Hennessy

Theos – enriching conversations

Theos exists to enrich the conversation about the role of faith in society.

Religion and faith have become key public issues in this century, nationally and globally. As our society grows more religiously diverse, we must grapple with religion as a significant force in public life. All too often, though, opinions in this area are reactionary or ill informed.

We exist to change this

We want to help people move beyond common misconceptions about faith and religion, behind the headlines and beneath the surface. Our rigorous approach gives us the ability to express informed views with confidence and clarity.

As the UK's leading religion and society think tank, we reach millions of people with our ideas. Through our reports, events and media commentary, we influence today's influencers and decision makers. According to *The Economist*, we're "an organisation that demands attention". We believe Christianity can contribute to the common good and that faith, given space in the public square, will help the UK to flourish.

Will you partner with us?

Theos receives no government, corporate or denominational funding. We rely on donations from individuals and organisations to continue our vital work. Please consider signing up as a Theos Friend or Associate or making a one off donation today.

Theos Friends and Students

— Stay up to date with our monthly newsletter

— Receive (free) printed copies of our reports

— Get free tickets to all our events

£75/ year
for Friends   **£40**/ year
for Students

Theos Associates

— Stay up to date with our monthly newsletter

— Receive (free) printed copies of our reports

— Get free tickets to all our events

— Get invites to private events with the Theos team and other Theos Associates

£375/ year

Sign up on our website:
www.theosthinktank.co.uk/about/support-us

Contents

Acknowledgements

I would like to record my thanks to the sponsors of the Edward Cadbury Lectures in the University of Birmingham, both for the invitation to give the lectures in 2016 that form this basis of this essay, and for their financial support towards the subsequent publication. I am equally grateful to Theos for agreeing to publish a revised edition of the lectures as a Theos essay.

An expanded version of Chapter 2 will appear in David Goodhew and Anthony-Paul Cooper (eds), *No Secular City: Church Growth and Decline in London, 1980 to the Present* (Routledge, forthcoming).

Grace Davie

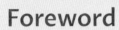

Foreword

In 1994 Grace Davie published her **Religion in Britain Since 1945** in association with the Institute of Contemporary British History, which Sir Anthony Seldon and I had co-founded in 1986. It was one of the most influential books in our "Making Contemporary Britain" series and its sub-title, "Believing Without Belonging", entered the mainstream of our national conversation about faith in the UK.

Grace possesses a very special gift. She excels at the spiritual equivalent of aerial photography. It's a very demanding art – perhaps the hardest of all of them that go into making a country's demographics. *Religion in Public Life: Levelling the Ground* is another very special Grace exposition, written with her customary clarity and lucidity based upon her Edward Cadbury Lectures delivered at the University of Birmingham in March 2016.

At a time of sharp anxiety about our country and the world we are fortunate to have a wise and good friend in Grace to guide us through the perplexities. She does this at both the micro and macro levels in an era which many regard as witnessing a return of religion as a big player in national and world affairs.

As in her 1994 study, Grace embeds her analysis in the context of wider social change in the UK and traces the development of what she calls "a model of choice, rather than a model of obligation or duty". This volume is a fascinating, stimulating new contribution to our conversation about the

spiritual and worshipping patterns of the nation and deserves
the widest readership and the most careful thought.

Peter Hennessy, FBA

Attlee Professor of Contemporary British History

Queen Mary University of London

Lord Hennessy of Nympsfield

September 2017

Introduction

In the early part of 2015, I was invited to give the 2016 Edward Cadbury Lectures in the University of Birmingham.[1] The invitation coincided with the establishment of the Edward Cadbury Centre for the Public Understanding of Religion, which exists within the University's Department of Theology and Religion. Its aim is "to enhance the public understanding of religion regionally, nationally and internationally through distinctive, strategic and engaged interdisciplinary research."[2] My lectures, which form the basis of this essay, reflected the goals of the Centre. They were delivered in March 2016.

Their overall title, "Religion in public life: Levelling the ground", was carefully chosen. It is a commonplace, nowadays, to say that religion has returned to public life. And like most commonplaces it is partially true. Religion is most certainly present in public life in new and highly visible ways but to imply that religion was once nowhere and is now everywhere is seriously misleading. We need instead to enquire carefully into the factors that have brought about the current shift in perspective. That done, we must examine in detail the different – and at times contrasting – ways in which religion manifests itself in the varied segments of society that we deem to be public.

I have chosen to tackle these questions by considering a series of 'levels', starting with the local and working up to the global – echoing (it so happens) the remit of Birmingham's new Centre. This is not a case of one size fits all. At the same time, I will pay particular attention to the notion of "religious literacy" – a frequently used term. Central to my argument will be the need to think more analytically about this concept, and then to discern which particular body of knowledge (and associated discourse) is appropriate at which 'level', recognising that the connections that emerge are very unlikely to be one-on-one relationships.

The first chapter, entitled "Thinking locally: continuity and change", develops the local case, underlining that the story is as much one of evolution as revolution. I use as my example, Exeter and the South West (my home) and pay particular attention to rural issues. What can and cannot be 'sustained' is a question that will be unpacked in some detail. It applies as much to the life of the churches as it does to the economy or the environment.

The second, "Rethinking the metropolis: the unexpected can and does happen", focuses on London. The empirical data, and the questions that they pose, are striking: gone are the supposedly negative associations between religion and urban life beloved of social science. Emerging instead is a vibrant religious market serving an ever more diverse city. An imaginative response is required.

The third chapter, "National conversations: whose feathers are ruffled?", looks at two national debates that have run in parallel from the late 1980s to the present day, and remain to a large extent unresolved. The first was triggered by *Faith in the City*; the second by Salman Rushdie's *The Satanic Verses*. A common theme is captured in the following question: whose feathers are ruffled when churches or faith communities intervene in public debate at national level?

The final chapter, "Global challenges: the contributions of social science", introduces a global initiative of which I was part. The International Panel on Social Progress (IPSP) brought together more than two hundred experts to deliver a report addressed to a wide range of social actors, movements, organisations, politicians, and decision-makers. The aim was to marshal the best possible expertise on questions that relate to social change.[3] The chapter relating to religion addressed two questions: what is the role of religion in terms of social progress and how can social science assist our understanding of this relationship? *Laudato si'*, Pope Francis' second encyclical on "Care for our Common Home", is taken as a case study.

A short conclusion draws the threads together and returns to the big picture. This includes: the sustainability (or otherwise) of current models, new (not always anticipated) opportunities, the 'turn' to religion, exceptional cases, and the need for innovative thinking in the social sciences. At the same time, it will take note of two world-changing events: Brexit and the election of President Trump, both of which have taken place since March 2016.

Both, moreover, pose questions for those who concern themselves with religion. For example: is it or is it not a coincidence that London displays indices of religious growth and votes massively to remain part of the European Union, and what is the place of migration in both these phenomena? The South West, conversely, struggles to sustain religious activity, votes to 'leave' and hosts very few migrants.

Meanwhile, President Trump's aspirations to ban migrants from named countries – all of which are majority Muslim – runs counter to the 'advice' that was presented in the IPSP chapter about how to manage diversity in a robust democracy.

Before embarking, it is important to recall, if only briefly, the shifting parameters of religion in this country, and indeed beyond. The full story can be found in my *Religion in Britain: A Persistent Paradox*.[4] This argues that there are six factors that are currently shaping the religious life of Britain, which not only change and adapt over time, but push and pull in different directions. The six factors are:

1   The role of the historic churches in forming British and indeed European culture. This is easily illustrated in the sense that the Christian tradition has had an enduring effect on time (calendars, seasons, festivals, holidays, weeks and weekends) and space (the parish system and the dominance of Christian buildings) in this part of the world.

2   Awareness that the historic churches still have a place at particular moments in the lives of British people, though they are no longer able to discipline the beliefs and behaviour of the great majority of people. Nor should they in a modern democracy where freedom of belief and the right to choose, join or leave a religion are paramount. Despite their relative secularity, however, a significant proportion of the population is likely to return to their churches at moments of celebration or grief (whether individual or collective).

3   An observable change in the churchgoing constituencies of this country, which operate increasingly on a model of choice, rather than a model of obligation or duty. As a result, membership of all churches is changing in nature; increasingly it is chosen rather than inherited, though more so in some places than in others. Organisational changes run parallel as a religious 'market' develops both within and without the historic churches.

4   The arrival into Britain of groups of people from many different parts of the world. This is primarily an economic movement, but the implications for religion are immense. The growing presence of Christians from the global South

alongside significant other faith communities has altered the religious profile of this country. Quite apart from this, some of these communities are – simply by their presence – challenging some deeply held assumptions, notably the notion that religion should be considered a private matter.

5   Rather different are the reactions of Britain's more secular voices to this shift: i.e. to the increasing significance of religion in public as well as private life. This growing constituency did not anticipate a shift of this nature, but its members now see it as their duty to question what is happening, sometimes aggressively, sometimes less so.

6   A gradual, but growing realisation that the patterns of religious life in modern Europe (including Britain) should be considered an 'exceptional case' – they are not a global prototype. It short, Europeans are beginning to realise that the part of the world in which they live is secular not because it is modern, but because it is has a particular – i.e. European – history. It is equally true that some European/British people welcome this insight; others are disconcerted by it.

It is important that we consider these factors alongside one another in order to get a rounded picture of what is happening. The future is uncertain. Indeed the current state of religion in Britain is paradoxical. On the one hand, religion has re-entered the public square and demands a response. On the other, a largely unchurched population has difficulty dealing with these issues in the sense that it is rapidly losing the concepts, knowledge and vocabulary that are necessary to talk well about religion. This is one reason for the lamentable standard of public debate in this field.

How can we manage this situation more constructively? That is the challenge facing our society today. My aim in this essay is to provide the building blocks for a better conversation about religion both in this country and in others. I will begin with issues that are most immediate to all of us.

My aim in this essay is to provide the building blocks for a better conversation about religion both in this country and in others.

[1]   These are funded by an endowment from the Cadbury Family to the University for an "annual series of lectures open to the public on the history, theology and culture of Christianity. They are hosted by the Department of Theology and Religion". The first series was given by Arnold Toynbee in 1948.

[2]   For more information, see *www.birmingham.ac.uk/schools/ptr/departments/theologyandreligion/research/cpur/index.aspx*

[3]   See *www.ipsp.org/aim*

[4]   Grace Davie, *Religion in Britain: A Persistent Paradox* (Wiley Blackwell, 2015).

1
Thinking locally:
continuity and change

To say that you are thinking locally immediate raises the question: local for whom? In this case it is local for me. My intention is to raise issues that resonate at regional or sub-regional level, using a particular example to make my case.

The far South West

I am not a 'native', but I have lived in Exeter for some 30 years and know the region (the South West) relatively well. In what follows I will concentrate on the counties of Devon and Cornwall; their predominantly rural nature is important for my argument. At the turn of the millennium, a visually striking publication brought together a huge amount of data on the sub-region presented in map form.[1] The scope of the volume was impressive and included sections on demography, political and military history, religion, education, agriculture, industry and mining, inland transport, maritime activities, towns and cities (Exeter and Plymouth), and tourism.

To select: Exeter is a Roman city (effectively the limit of the Roman Empire) and is the seat of the Bishop of Exeter whose jurisdiction covered the counties of Devon and Cornwall until the formation of the Diocese of Truro in 1876, this being very nearly coterminous with the county of Cornwall. Plymouth is a naval city, from which Sir Francis Drake set out to defeat the Spanish Armada in 1588, and from which – some 30 years later – the Pilgrim Fathers departed for America. Both cities were bombed in World War II – Exeter in a Baedecker raid in April/May 1942,[2] and Plymouth mercilessly from 1941-44 given the presence of the dockyard. Currently their economic fortunes are somewhat different: Plymouth is a much bigger city (some 260,000 people) but less prosperous than its smaller but expanding neighbour (circa 125,000). Exeter's demography is the mirror image of the surrounding region. More generally, economic fortunes deteriorate the further west that you go. Cornwall's economy is largely dependent upon agriculture and tourism. It is one of the poorest areas in the United Kingdom qualifying (with only three others) for poverty-related grants from the European Social Fund.

The religious profiles of Cornwall and Devon are distinctive. Historically, both contained significant non-conformist populations, but in different proportions. In Devon, this was relatively varied in terms of denomination; in Cornwall, it was dominated by Methodism with all its internal diversity. Bruce Coleman's account of the 1851 Census of Religious Worship provides a benchmark.[3] Devon was not so very different, in terms of its overall figures, from the counties of its division and region. Cornwall, in contrast, was *sui generis*, characterised by strong nonconformity and remarkably weak Anglicanism. That said, the effective division between the two counties was not the county boundary. There were rather three sub-regions. The first was Devon east of Dartmoor, where Anglicanism was strong, old dissent well established, and Methodist connections modest. The second comprised west Devon and east Cornwall, where Anglicanism and old dissent ceded place to diverse forms of Methodism, notably Bible Christians. In the west of Cornwall, Methodism was rampant.[4]

Generational change

These underlying patterns persisted through much of the 20th century penetrating the world of politics as well as religion, in spite of marked secularisation. As late as the 1980s statistically significant correlations could still be found between the presence of Methodism in both counties and the Liberal vote.[5] As the century came to an end, however, things were beginning to change. First, it was becoming clear that the parish model of the established church was – relatively speaking – more resilient than free-church congregations, bearing in mind that some of the latter are more secure than others.[6] Far more radical was the shift that constitutes a thread running right through these chapters: the gradual realisation that rural churches no longer do 'better' overall than urban ones. The former, moreover, are living on borrowed time in the sense that they are disproportionately sustained by a generation that is passing.

Crucial in this respect is to admire what this generation – and in particular the women within it – have achieved (and still do achieve) against significant odds.[7] It is largely thanks to them that churches and chapels continue in existence and serve the communities of which they are part. To keep on talking about the dearth of younger people is understandable, but is at times insensitive. To be continually reminded of the sections of the population who are not there undervalues those who are. And to keep on changing things with a view to attracting newcomers (i.e. 'young people') can – if you are not careful – result in a double negative: not only do you achieve little but you strain existing loyalties.

So what is to be done? In what follows I start by considering the challenges facing rural churches, including those in the South West. I then turn to a number of local initiatives, foregrounding the impressive – but often undocumented – achievements of religiously active people of all kinds, many of which reach out into the community. Two of these pay particular attention to 'religious literacy'. The final paragraphs affirm a more general point, that is the role of the *local* media, noting that frequently local papers and local radio or television are markedly more positive towards religious initiatives than their national equivalents.

Challenges and achievements

The data that emerged from the 'religious' questions in the 2001 and 2011 British censuses have attracted widespread attention. This is not the place to examine these findings in detail but to note the gradual, but increasingly visible, rebalancing that they reveal between urban and rural contexts. Census data, moreover, can be supplemented by more detailed findings from the churches themselves,[8] leading to the following conclusion. All parts of the country are subject to secularisation, as 'traditional' forms of religion continue to decline, but the opportunities for compensatory growth (i.e. the success stories of a growing market in religion) are more present in the city than they are in rural areas – a fact very largely explained by the key role of migration in this process, and nowhere more so than in London (a story told in Chapter 2).

> **All parts of the country are subject to secularisation, but the opportunities for compensatory growth are more present in the city than they are in rural areas.**

In the meantime, the rural churches find themselves in a difficult situation: the erosion continues, but with little in the way of compensation. The consequences are all too clear: a diminishing constituency is responsible for an infrastructure that is too large to sustain. Closures are inevitable especially among the free churches. The evidence is there for all to see as the buildings in question are transformed into secular amenities, local businesses or private houses. A parochially-based established church is in a rather different position given its commitment to universal presence, that is, availability at the point of need to those living in a designated place. Such an arrangement has many advantages, not least stability. All kinds of things decline in rural areas: post-offices, shops, schools, pubs, chapels even – but the parish church remains. But how is this church, and the ministry it sustains, to be maintained as the resources required to do this erode along with the actively faithful?

A point to note is the very fine line between something which is stable (i.e. an entity that holds firm in difficult circumstances) and something that is static (i.e. an organisation that is incapable of adaptation). For adapt the church must to ensure a continuing presence. Such a situation calls for the clearest possible thinking about what in the inherited model is worth sustaining and what is not. The question can be directed to buildings, many of which are of architectural value, to working practices and to personnel. The dioceses of the far South West are not the only ones to be faced with such dilemmas; they do however exemplify them sharply.

Much more positive are the extraordinary number of initiatives that are sustained, despite everything. Take, for example, those that emanate from the Church and Society Office of the Diocese of Exeter.[9] These include a cluster of economic concerns, relating to the living wage, credit unions, community currencies and green economics; food issues such as food banks and food poverty; ecology and the environment, including eco-churches, renewables and divestment; health and well-being, including dementia workshops and dementia champions, mental health issues and disability; interfaith work (both presence and engagement); and social justice, that is fair-trade, trafficking and – increasingly – refugees. Such initiatives are sustained, as they are elsewhere, by countless volunteers giving generously of their time, talents and money to raise awareness, to offer assistance, and to advocate for those in need.

It is activities such as these, moreover, that constitute the nitty gritty of the data that emerged from two pan-European studies of welfare and religion in Europe carried out in the first decade of the 21st century.[10] These covered a wide variety of European countries, but were effectively locality studies in that the core unit of analysis was a medium sized town (one in each participating country). The stand-out finding right across Europe was the mismatch between the increasing demands made on churches and other faith-based organisations as the welfare state erodes, or – more accurately – fails to keep up with the ever-increasing demands of an ageing population, and the fortunes of the organisations themselves. This leads us to an inescapable conclusion: more is asked of less in the west of England just as it is in localities all over Europe – and for exactly the same reasons: demand exceeds supply, an excess exacerbated by restricted public spending.[11]

Correcting stereotypes

All that said, context matters. Take, for example, questions of social justice in the South West. We can pick up the story in 1992, the publication date of "'Keep Them in Birmingham': Challenging Racism in South-west England", a Commission for Racial Equality report, which covered the counties of Cornwall, Devon, Dorset, and Somerset.[12] This painted a disturbing picture of prejudice and discrimination directed against the relatively few ethnic minority residents either visiting or living in this part of the country at the time. The data were shocking, revealing a toxic combination of discrimination, condescension and bigotry. In terms of responses and reactions from a wide variety of organisations (information, employment, social services, education, further and higher education, careers services, police, trade unions and tourist boards), the short sections relating to the churches are interesting. On the one hand, they indicated significant levels of activity designed to help congregations understand and oppose racism. On the other, they demonstrated an acute awareness that such activities were barely scratching the surface. For example: an Anglican bishop wrote bluntly that what his church was doing was "very little or nothing", because his diocese was "an area which thinks there is no problem".[13] Widespread complacency, bordering on denial, lay at the root of the problem.

How much has changed since the early 1990s? There are certainly hopeful signs in, for example, the designations of a number of places in the South West as "cities of sanctuary" (not all of them urban).[14] More worrying was the continuing hostility towards migrants expressed by at least some 'leave' voters in the 2016 United Kingdom European Union membership referendum.[15] One point, however, is clear: the terms of the debate have evolved since the 1980s, away from racial or ethnic issues *per se* and towards religion and religious differences, a shift to be discussed in more detail in chapters 2 and 3, and one in which the need for an improved religious literacy is central.

In the far South West, two initiatives catch the eye in this respect. The first is the Plymouth Centre for Faiths and Cultural Diversity (PCFCD), established in 2001 in order to create opportunities for children and young people to meet speakers from a variety of faiths and cultural backgrounds.[16] The Centre was a response to a perceived need across the city for a greater awareness of the multi-faith and multicultural society in which we live. It is now considered a major resource, "providing contacts, expertise and experience within the fields of religious diversity, interfaith dialogue and support and engagement with faith communities". It deploys and trains 'faith speakers' who are people of faith/culture who want to share their experiences with pupils. Sessions or workshops in the classroom or in assemblies are tailored to the needs of particular schools. Central to this work is a growing awareness that children who grow up in a part of the country where the presence of other faiths is relatively limited must acquire knowledge and sensitivities in this area just like anyone else – indeed more so given their lack of everyday inter-faith or inter-cultural encounters.

The same is true of Learn, Teach, Lead RE (LTLRE), which exists to improve the quality of Religious Education in all schools in the region.[17] LTLRE is a learning partnership project, which aims to create "a community of enquiry and professional development". It works with all teachers of RE irrespective of their experience or qualifications, and does this through hands-on support at hub meetings. Such support includes the opportunity to participate in projects that develop not only the skills of teachers but the learning experiences of their pupils. In addition, all participants are invited to an annual conference, which has become a springboard for further action. Partnership, encouragement and collaboration lie at the heart of the model. For example, specially-trained hub leaders are themselves teachers striving to develop their own practice as well as the skills of those that they work with.

Feedback from these various activities reveals that LTLRE affiliates have raised their expectations of what pupils can achieve in RE; become more aware of how their teaching affects pupils' learning and progress in RE; been successful in implementing new teaching approaches; and acquired new subject knowledge. Even more pleasing have been external reactions to this initiative, as its participants increasingly take part in national debates about RE. One consequence is that

LTLRE offshoots are beginning to appear in other parts of the country.[18]

A final point concerns an often overlooked aspect of the media in so far as they relate to religion. Such inter-relationships constitute a burgeoning field given the variety of outlets covered by the term 'media', and the different ways in which each participant in this ongoing interaction influences the other. The 'conversation' can be fractious to say the least. Frequently omitted from the picture, however, is the distinctive place of *local* media, which are noticeably more balanced in their accounts of religion and religious activities than their national equivalents. They are, it seems, able to resist to a greater degree the temptation (indeed the pressure) to attract readership or audiences by focusing more on conflict, deviance and celebrity than is helpful.[19] The reason lies in the proximity of local reporters to their sources, in the sense that knowledge is likely to be based on verifiable accounts from known (and trusted) individuals.

Take, for instance, the following example from Exeter's *Express and Echo*, written in connection with "Visit my mosque day" in February 2017. To be fair, the national coverage of this event was for the most part positive, coming as it did right after Donald Trump announced the prohibition on individuals travelling to the United States from seven Muslim-majority countries and the total ban on Syrian refugees, not to mention a shooting in a mosque in Québec City. That said, the piece in the *Express and Echo* is strikingly informative, entirely positive and very well written.[20] It gives details of the mosque itself, its history, and its role in the community; at the same time it explains what goes on inside the building and the reasons for this. The volunteer tour guide (a woman) suggests – tactfully – that the media are not always the best guide to the nature of

Islam. Far better is first-hand experience and a visit to the local mosque and its personnel as was the case for the journalist in question. The article concludes by underlining the positive reception that Muslims have in the local community, in this case Exeter.

An earlier piece from the same paper (1 November 2016) was provoked by a serious fire in the centre of the city; its content is interesting in that it joins together a number of threads in this chapter.[21] As a result of the road closures brought about by the fire, the normal Wednesday night soup kitchen for the homeless was not able to take place in the Cathedral. A team from the mosque stepped in to provide what was necessary, affirming a partnership already in place. The normality of it all was the essential point: the roles of faith communities in providing for the homeless on a regular basis; the partnership between different faiths in maintaining this service; and the need to continue despite a devastating fire in the neighbourhood.

> Faith communities offer a unique combination in terms of social action: an ethic of care embedded in their teaching and an unrivalled network of opportunities through which to express this.

Sustainable or not?

In short, the article exemplifies the continuity and change found in the religious life of countless localities in this country. Time-honoured activities continue, but in different ways and supported by different – increasingly diverse – groups of people, many of them unpaid. For which reason, the effective use of volunteers becomes a key element. Used creatively volunteers can sustain a multiplicity of actions and activities; pushed too far they – and the institutions of which they are part – crack under the strain. One point, however, is clear. Faith communities offer a unique combination in terms of social action: an ethic of care embedded in their teaching and an unrivalled network of opportunities through which to express this.[22] The results are impressive. But is this way of working sustainable in the longer term given the erosion of the institutions that lie behind it? The significance of this question will be reiterated in the conclusion.

[1] Roger Kain and William Ravenhill (eds), *Historical Atlas of South-West England* (University of Exeter Press, 1999).

[2] The nature of the Baedecker raids is explained in *www.iwm.org.uk/history/what-were-the-baedeker-raids*

[3] Bruce Coleman, 'Religious worship in 1851', in Kain and Ravenhill, *Historical Atlas* (1999), pp. 228-33.

[4] Ibid. p. 229.

[5] See Grace Davie, *Religion in Britain since 1945: Believing without Belonging* (Blackwell, 1994), and Grace Davie and Derek Hearl, 'Religion and ecclesiastical practices in the twentieth century', in Kain and Ravenhill, *Historical Atlas* (1999), pp. 234-39.

[6] Michael Winter, 'The twentieth century. Part 1 Cornwall', in Nicholas Orme (ed.), *Unity and Diversity: A History of the Church in Devon and Cornwall* (University of Exeter Press, 1991), pp. 157-74. The rapid decline in Methodism is well documented both nationally and locally – see, for example, *www.methodist.org.uk/mission/statistics-for-mission*

[7] For more information, see Abby Day, *The Religious Lives of Older Laywomen: The Last Active Anglican Generation* (Oxford University Press, 2017).

[8] See for example the regularly updated statistics for the Church of England, broken down by dioceses. Available at: *www.churchofengland.org/about-us/facts-stats/research-statistics/statistics-for-mission.aspx*

[9] This is a field in which individuals matter. The range and variety of the activities covered in the Diocese of Exeter owes a great deal to the energies and experience of the current Church and Society and Environment Officer, Martyn Goss. Martyn has been endlessly helpful in supplying relevant information. See also *exeter.anglican.org/resources/faith-action/*

[10] These are 'Welfare and Religion in a European Perspective' and 'Welfare and Values in Europe'. See in particular Anders Bäckström and Grace Davie with Ninna Edgardh and Per Pettersson (eds), *Welfare and Religion in 21st Century Europe (Volume 1): Configuring the Connections* (Ashgate, 2010), Anders Bäckström, Grace Davie, Ninna Edgardh and Per Pettersson (eds), *Welfare and Religion in 21st Century Europe (Volume 2): Gendered, Religious and Social Change* (Ashgate, 2011) and Lina Molokotos-Liederman, with Anders Bäckström and Grace Davie (eds), *Religion and Welfare in Europe: Gendered and Minority Perspectives* (Policy Press, 2017).

[11] See also Nick Spencer, *Doing Good: A Future for Christianity in the 21st Century* (Theos, 2016).

12 Eric Jay, '"Keep them in Birmingham": Challenging Racism in South-west England' (Commission for Racial Equality, 1992). An electronic version is available at: *plymouthanddevonrec.org.uk/images/keep%20them%20in%20 birmingham.pdf*

13 Ibid. p. 31.

14 For more information about cities of sanctuary, see *cityofsanctuary.org/about/*

15 The regional breakdowns for the referendum result are available at: *ig.ft. com/sites/elections/2016/uk/eu-referendum/*. The strength of the leave vote in the South West was clearly evident but less marked than that in the East of England.

16 For more information, see *www.pcfcd.co.uk/*

17 For more information, see *ltlre.org/*

18 Substantial funding from the Jerusalem Trust has enabled LTLRE to extend its work into three other south western areas. A similar initiative has also begun in the North West (see *www.ltlre-north.org/*).

19 For an excellent overview of religion and the media see Kim Knott, Elizabeth Poole and Teemu Taira, *Media Portrayals of Religion and the Secular Sacred* (Ashgate, 2013).

20 '"Visit my mosque day" – A tour inside one of Exeter's most beautiful holy buildings', *Devon Live* 5 February 2017. This article is no longer available on the Devon Live website, but the text can be viewed here: *africanewswire.za.com/ visit-my-mosque-day-a-tour-inside-one-of-exeters-most-3/*

21 The substance of this article can be found on: *www.anglicannews.org/ news/2016/11/mosque-steps-in-to-feed-homeless-as-fire-forces-continued-closure-of-exeter-cathedral.aspx*

22 The work of Robin Gill elaborates the significance of this combination. See his *Moral Communities* (University of Exeter Press, 1992) and *Churchgoing and Christian Ethics* (Cambridge University Press, 1999). A question should be asked, however, about younger generations whose networks depend more on social media than face to face encounters.

2
Rethinking the metropolis: the unexpected can and does happen

In the mid-20th century, London was considered a beacon of secular thinking. That is no longer the case, at least not exclusively so. The change became increasingly visible as the century drew to a close, since when London has become an area of noticeable religious growth whilst retaining elements of its distinctive secularity. Much of the growth is driven by new arrivals, but not all – innovative thinking across a variety of religious organisations has resulted in positive outcomes for many. One way to grasp what is happening is to appreciate that London is no longer a European city. It is exhibiting instead the features of the gateway or global city that it has become.

A visual representation taken from the 2011 census illustrates the point (see Figure 2:1, below).[1] It depicts the regions of England and Wales as these are constituted for the census. Simply a glance at the figure reveals that London is distinctive. The bar chart displays unequivocally both the rapidly growing religious diversity of the capital and the relative lack of those who claim 'no religious attachment'. The former was expected; the latter less so. Self-affiliating Christians are also fewer in number than is the case in other regions but – as will become clear in this chapter – they tend to be more active in their faith than their co-religionists elsewhere.

It is worth noting in passing that the profile of the South West is quite different: here there are noticeably higher levels of 'no religious attachment', a larger proportion of self-affiliating Christians, and modest – very modest – levels of diversity.

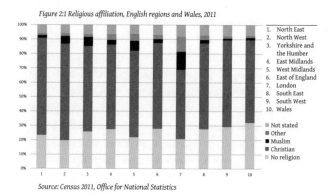

Figure 2:1 Religious affiliation, English regions and Wales, 2011

1. North East
2. North West
3. Yorkshire and the Humber
4. East Midlands
5. West Midlands
6. East of England
7. London
8. South East
9. South West
10. Wales

■ Not stated
■ Other
■ Muslim
■ Christian
■ No religion

Source: Census 2011, Office for National Statistics

Keeping this picture in mind, this chapter proceeds as follows. It begins by revisiting the six factors presented in the Introduction, asking to what extent they still resonate in the London case. The subsequent discussion deploys different types of data to fill out the picture. The first section sets out the statistical profiles, both Christian and other faiths. The second describes a broad swathe of city life encompassing the highly visible diversity of Tower Hamlets at one end and Islington's developed secularity at the other. This is the Stepney Episcopal Area of the Diocese of London. The third draws from a study of London's megachurches – a relatively new form of religious life – and the fourth looks at selected aspects of the capital's cathedrals.

The six factors applied to London

Does the distinctiveness of London mean that the six factors no longer apply? That is not the case. They do however need rebalancing.

Clearly the cultural heritage continues to exist: the rhythm of the working week remains the same, and the parishes of the Church of England are still present, lying beneath – and working with – the myriad activities of many different faiths that take place both within and across their boundaries. It is still a challenge for the Anglican Dioceses (of London and Southwark) to sustain this network, though the former is doing noticeably well on most of the conventional indicators.[2] A comprehensive account of this work can be found in the then Bishop of London's Lambeth Lecture on church growth in the capital, delivered in September 2015.[3] The start date for this retrospect is 1990, when "the decline in the active membership of the Church of England as a whole in the last quarter of the 20th century was mirrored and exaggerated in London". The change in mood as the indicators begin to turn up is palpable.

De facto many Anglican parishes become themselves part of the market that is London, whether in religion or in anything else. And as expected, choice abounds. Congregations emerge both within and without the established church to meet very different needs: of language and ethnicity, of profession and predilection (actors, artists and journalists etc.), of musical styles, of churchmanship and spirituality, of tradition and innovation, of gender and sexualities, of families and friendship groups. Almost no one assumes that 'people' will attend, still less join, these gatherings out of a sense of obligation or duty, but attend they will if the religious community in question makes it worth their while. It is equally clear that the most obvious gainers in the current religious mix – the many and varied charismatic churches and the cathedrals – exist in abundance in the capital (see below).

It is well recognised that the upswing in the religious indicators in London is significantly stimulated by the migrants who continue to arrive in the city. Indeed, for many of them a religious congregation or its equivalent is a central feature of their journeying, in terms of motivation, welcome and assimilation. This was not always the case. Indeed the historic churches have much to regret in their failure to welcome the Afro-Caribbeans who arrived in the immediate post-war period. Formed by the missionary churches in their own countries, the newcomers were cold-shouldered by many English Christians who preferred their own rather staid habits to the exuberance of their 'visitors'. Unsurprisingly, the latter took their custom elsewhere, setting up increasing numbers of Afro-Caribbean churches which became some of the most vibrant in the market. Those of other faiths did likewise, establishing a huge variety of prayer rooms, mosques, gurdwaras, and temples, making London one of the most religiously diverse cities in West Europe. The foregrounding of faith in this story, which was initially articulated in terms of race, ethnicity and culture, is as true – if not truer – in London as it is elsewhere.

The turn to religion brings with it new understandings of the secular as well as the religious. These perceptions vary in nature. On the one hand are 'secularists' who support the idea of 'neutral' space in which expressions of faith are welcomed alongside everyone else; on the other are those that reject this possibility on principle. In short, the secular – just like religion – can vary from the generous and accommodating to the excluding and exclusive; and – once again just like religion – the secular doesn't simply exist as a concept but takes root in particular spaces, both geographical and social. London is host to both growing religion and innovative forms of the secular, and often in close proximity.

The final factor introduced the notion of exceptionality in terms of Europe. The same question can be addressed to London. Is the religious growth of London a sign of things to come, or is it an exceptional case in British terms? The question should be kept in mind in the reading of this chapter. It will be raised once again in the conclusion.

Statistical profiles

Peter Brierley's London Church Census was a wide-ranging survey of London's churches carried out in 2012 and published a year later.[4] The opening sentences of the summary report catch the eye:

> Church attendance has grown from just over 620,000 in 2005 to just over 720,000 in the 7 years to 2012, a 16% increase. Nowhere else in the UK has attendance grown so dramatically. While these numbers are across all denominations, the growth is especially seen in the Black Majority Churches (Pentecostals) and the various Immigrant Churches (Smaller Denominations).[5]

It is important to see these remarks in context: the growth may or may not continue and the increase in attendance is almost entirely due to relatively high levels of immigration in the capital. Rising levels of religious activity need moreover to be set against a decline in the proportion of London's population declaring itself Christian, from 58% in 2001 to 48% in 2011 – noting, however, that over the period this fall was the smallest of any region in the country.

All that said, the detail in Brierley's report and the initiatives that lie behind this make startling reading for those accustomed to a narrative of decline. For example, between 2005 and 2012, on average two new congregations opened every week in Greater London (making 100 each year) – a 17% increase, and a number projected to rise by a further 5% in the next eight years. Putting the same point in a different way, Brierley tells us that 300 existing churches in London closed in the seven years following 2005, whereas some 1,000 new ones were set up. Of these new churches, 93% were still in existence after five years, against a 76% survival rate elsewhere.

Two thirds of these were Pentecostal black-majority churches and one third were catering for a particular language or ethnic group (the diversity is endless). The growth, moreover, is disproportionately female (heavily so), but the age distribution is more balanced in London than it is in most places. Congregation size is significant in this respect; larger churches grow faster than smaller ones and attract more young people. Pentecostal churches multiply fastest of all and in 2012 accounted for 32% of London's churchgoers. The question of leadership is significant: the great majority of churches in London (including the Anglicans) have the privilege of a priest or pastor exclusively for that church, in marked contrast to the rest of the country where this is increasingly rare, especially in rural areas. That privilege implies that there is sufficient funding to sustain a more favourable ratio. Money matters.

So much for the Christians. Between 2001 and 2011, the percentages of Londoners identifying with the major other-faith communities grew (or not) as follows: Muslims from 8.5% to 12.4%, Hindus from 4% to 5%, Buddhists from 0.8% to 1.0% and others from 0.5% to 0.6%. The percentage of Jews fell from 2% to 1.8%, and the Sikhs remain unchanged at 1.5%. Residential patterns are highly significant in this respect: different faith communities live in different parts of the capital. Detailed information about these clusters can be gleaned from the census, tracked over time, and mapped against a multitude of other variables.[6] Distinctive patterns emerge.

Nowhere is the diversity more noticeable than in London's east end, which over several centuries has welcomed Huguenot

Protestants, European Jews, Irish Catholics, Bengali and Somali Muslims, Chinese Buddhists, and many others. Buildings adapt accordingly. Take for example the *Jamme Masjid* (Great Mosque) in Brick Lane which was initially built in 1743 as a Protestant chapel *(La Neuve Eglise)* for the Huguenot community. In 1809, it was bought by the (then) London Society for Promoting Christianity Amongst the Jews; a decade later it became a Methodist chapel. In the late 19th century, the building responded to a different need, becoming Spitalfields' Great Synagogue in order to serve the growing number of Jewish refugees arriving from Russia and East Europe. A century later (in the mid-1970s) it changed again to become a mosque for the expanding Bangladeshi community that had settled in the area.

The Stepney episcopal area

The Diocese of London is divided into five Episcopal Areas. One of these will be taken as an example to illustrate the diversity of experience which is London. The Stepney Episcopal Area covers the London boroughs of Hackney, Islington and Tower Hamlets – an area which includes huge social and economic contrasts.

Alan Piggot's "Contextual survey of the Stepney Episcopal Area" is an excellent resource in this respect, the more so in that it contains a series of maps depicting the distribution of ethnic as well as religious groups across the three boroughs that make up the Episcopal Area.[7] Regarding ethnicity, the clustered presence of the Bangladeshi community in Tower Hamlets is striking, a fact which accounts for the high percentage of Muslims and the relatively low proportion of Christians in the borough. Regarding religion, confined in the "Contextual survey" mapping to Christian and no-religion, it is possible to 'see' the percentage of the latter rising as you move north and west.

The survey was commissioned by the Area Bishop as a background to the work of the Anglican Church in Stepney: it is concerned with vision as well as context and considers the area as a whole rather than its sub-units (deaneries or parishes). Immediately striking are the challenges facing a parochially organised church in a part of London undergoing exceptionally rapid change, not least the creation of the Olympic Park. Equally interesting is the fact that the data are set in a longer term time-line than is often the case, which puts into perspective more recent shifts in population. For example, "in 1911, there were 165 Stepney parishes serving a population of some 1.4 million, giving an average parish population of around 8,500. Currently, there are 63 parishes for a population of just over half the 1911 total, with an average parish population of around 11,300."[8] Quite apart, that is, from the multiplicity of new churches existing in the area – among which are seven Anglican initiatives.[9]

The core question cannot, however, be avoided: how is it possible to deploy creatively structures which – simply by what they are – emphasise historical and geographical consistency over longish periods of time? Is it sensible even to try? The data in this case indicate that it is – a statement strongly supported by evidence from *Another Capital Idea: Church Growth in the Diocese of London 2003-2010*, which indicates that growth across the Diocese is noticeably higher in inner London, including the Stepney Episcopal Area, than it is further out.[10] It is also worth noting that the Stepney Area sustains 29 Church of England voluntary aided schools, of which 26 are primary and three secondary. Its ministries, moreover, reach into the many and varied secular institutions (universities, hospitals and prisons etc.) located in the area.

Hackney and Islington (together with its neighbour Camden) house a very different constituency: here a significant section of the population reports having 'no religion' – a feature that merits our attention. As we have seen, 'non-religion' is growing as a category across the country; so – unsurprisingly – are academic studies of this. Insightful in this respect are Lois Lee's analyses of the topic.[11] Specifically, her writing brings together sophisticated theorising and careful empirical work to articulate an important shift in emphasis: away from what she calls the hollowly secular to the substantively non-religious, recognising the latter as a lived and essentially social reality, not simply a reasoned and individualised epistemology.

How is this expressed in North London? An obvious starting point is the Sunday Assembly with its initial sites in Islington and Hackney, followed by a move to Conway Hall (an ethical society of long standing) in Camden. The Sunday Assembly is in fact a hybrid which is religious in form but secular in content, making it very difficult to place on a continuum. Does this represent the notion of a religious market taken to its logical conclusion, or is it something entirely distinct, best seen in a long tradition of freethinking? Particularly interesting in terms of the latter is Lee's awareness that this initiative alongside others – the British Humanist Association, the Atheist Bus Campaign, Alain de Botton's School of Life – all enjoy close proximity in a relatively small area of north London. This in turn reflects a more general finding from the census: i.e. that like-minded people tend to cluster in particular areas, forming what Voas and McAndrew call non-religious 'microclimates'.[12] Islington and Camden, with their developed tradition of middle-class, well-educated and secular-minded thinking, are one such.

London's megachurches

Entirely different is the phenomenon known as megachurches, currently the subject of a research project housed in the Cadbury Centre for the Public Understanding of Religion in Birmingham.[13] Megachurches, as the name implies, are defined in terms of numbers – they are those with a congregation of 2,000 or more. Though relatively common in the United States, and even more so in the global south, congregations of this size represent an unexpected turn in the religious life of 21st century Britain. Here, then, is further evidence for categorising London as a global city rather than a European one.

> "
> When does 'betterment' become 'prosperity' and who is to decide where the line is drawn?

Out of an initial pool of ten or eleven such churches, the project team have studied five in depth. The first 'set' is made up of three Nigerian-led congregations. These were drawn from six similar churches located in different parts of London.[14] As its title suggests, the "Megachurches and Social Engagement in London" project concentrates on a particular theme within their work. The social engagement in question is expressed both in individual lives and community enterprise, the goal being to improve the life chances of all those that come into contact with these organisations. Particularly interesting in this respect are the sometimes conflicting value judgements that abound in this field. To give but one example: captured by the old-fashioned term 'betterment', the work of such churches is deemed entirely beneficial, but as soon as such activities tip over into the endorsement of 'prosperity', they are seen as contentious. But when does 'betterment' become 'prosperity' and who is to decide where the line is drawn? Whatever the answer given, it is undeniable that enterprises of this size generate significant amounts of social capital – both bonding and bridging – in the neighbourhoods of which they are part, a theme that will unfold as the project moves to completion.

In the meantime, it is worth noting that two of the megachurches selected for this study are Anglican and – to that extent – are part of the parish system. Both however function very largely as gathered churches, drawing like-minded people from different parts of London and indeed beyond. The first – Holy Trinity Brompton (HTB) – is a well-known charismatic church and the home base for Alpha.[15] It is located in South Kensington and attracts around 4,500 worshippers over eleven services in a week. This is not the place for a detailed examination of HTB's many and varied activities, but it is worth highlighting two points. First, the church epitomises one of the 'success stories' of the growing religious market in this country outlined in the introduction; it is, however, larger and more extensive than most others. And second, HTB is the initiator of a number of the church plants in the Stepney Episcopal Area – the joined-up thinking is important.

The multicultural congregation gathered in Langham Place sustains one of the largest church-based ministries for homeless people in central London.

The second example has a longer history. It is All Souls' Langham Place, where John Stott – one of the best known evangelicals of the 20th century – was present for more than five decades. Less well-known is the fact that the multicultural congregation gathered in Langham Place sustains one of the largest church-based ministries for homeless people in central London, working through the All Souls Local Action Network (or ASLAN for short). Aggregating its ministries, ASLAN makes more than 200 interventions each week, and over 10,000 each year, in the lives of homeless and vulnerably housed people in London. In addition the church is engaged locally in anti-trafficking initiatives, care for sex workers, student work, sports programmes, youth clubs, after-school clubs, toddler and baby groups and care for the elderly. The range of activities is striking.

> **The notion of 'conditionality' exists more in the mind than it does on the ground.**

In both HTB and All Souls, the question of proselytism is not only central to their social engagement but contentious. As one of the researchers indicates, it is central to everything that goes on in these churches. Indeed, it would be a "misunderstanding of the context of a church to expect them to contribute to society by providing a service without proselytising. To do so would be to undermine their central vision, their theological motivations for volunteering and their key mechanism for helping people".[16] Such an approach, however, is contentious in that care – it seems – comes with strings attached. But is this the case?

The data from this project suggest that it is not, a finding consistently endorsed in the literature on faith-based welfare.[17] It appears that the notion of 'conditionality' exists more in the mind than it does on the ground. There is, however, a body of opinion – held by significant numbers of Britain's secularists – that the provision of welfare is the responsibility of the state rather than the churches and should be a strictly secular affair. That's fine in principle but the key question remains unanswered: what is to be done when the state in question is unable to meet this obligation?[18]

Cathedral life

Cathedrals exemplify a further category of large churches, which is both similar to and different from those already described. They are similar in the sense that they attract sizeable gathered congregations, sometimes from an extensive geographical area, but they are different in that they are quintessentially European. Historically these buildings towered over the cities of which they were part. Less dominant physically in London than they used to be (the Shard dwarfs St Paul's despite it being one of the largest cathedrals in the world), they remain key players in the religious economy of the capital.

The literature on the growing importance of cathedrals in England as a whole is now extensive.[19] There are many reasons for their relative success. Among them is a range of what might be called aesthetic or liturgical features: the beauty of the building, the music (frequently world class), the pattern of the liturgy and the quality of preaching, all of which bring different 'categories' of people to cathedrals. Such people include regular and less regular worshippers, pilgrims and tourists, bearing in mind that the lines between these activities are evidently porous. A further variable is, however, crucial: that is the relative anonymity of cathedrals as interested or simply curious individuals are allowed to come and go as they please, without having to 'sign up' for further commitment or continued attendance. Such anonymity, and the freedom that comes with it, is clearly attractive to significant sections of the population.

The London cathedrals are no different in this respect, except that they operate on a larger scale than many (if not all) of their equivalents elsewhere.[20] One further point, however, needs emphasis – that is the very considerable convening power of these institutions which are able to bring together an unusually wide range of individuals, many of whom 'represent' the diverse elements of London life. Take as evidence the work of the Westminster Abbey Institute or its equivalent at St Paul's Cathedral, and consider the kinds of people involved, the organisations that they represent, the audiences reached, the range of topics addressed, and the debates generated. The scope of this work is impressive and the echo wide.[21] Equally memorable was the consternation of the general public when St Paul's was temporarily closed due to health and safety concerns at the time of the Occupy London Movement in 2011. This is not the place to debate the rights and wrongs of the decision to close the building, still less the Occupy Movement itself. More important is the taken-for-granted nature of access to the cathedral – hence the dismay when it was unexpectedly denied.[22]

Southwark Cathedral is less well known than its equivalents north of the river. That said, it played host to a notably positive episode in the summer of 2016, when the newly-elected London mayor, Sadiq Khan (who happened to be a Muslim), was formally signed in to his new role there, enthusiastically welcomed by Londoners of all kinds (Christian, other faith and no faith). The mayor grew up on a housing estate just a few miles from the cathedral.

A rather different example completes this section. Westminster Cathedral is the seat of the Cardinal Archbishop of Westminster and the Mother Church for Roman Catholics in England and Wales. As such it gathers a truly global community. An instance that underlines the 'reach' of the Catholic Church in this respect is the high profile Mass for Migrants, which has become an annual event organised jointly by the Diocese of Westminster, the Archdiocese of Southwark and the Diocese of Brentwood. All three – and to a degree the dioceses right across the country – are increasingly aware of new arrivals in the Catholic community. In 2016, as in previous years, the Mass began with the banner procession, in itself an indication of the rich diversity of the Catholic community in London. The service remembered the increasing numbers of refugees and migrants around the world, who have been obliged to leave their homes because of political unrest or economic turmoil, and who struggle against the odds to gain a foothold in a sometimes hostile environment.[23]

Interestingly, Peter Brierley also remarks on the growing diversity of the Catholic population, noting in particular churches that cater for different language communities. Equally fascinating is Alana Harris' 'portrait' of a Catholic parish in Canning Town.[24] This was founded in the mid-19th century as a hub for Irish immigrants seeking work in the east end – an entirely familiar story. In the early 21st century, the congregation is not only still there but thriving. It has also changed in nature: approximately 1,200 people gather on a Sunday morning from more than 40 migrant backgrounds. The specific contributions of Catholics from the Philippines, the West Indies and different parts of Africa are explored in detail in a study which documents the return to Britain of habits originally exported by missionaries. The process is re-animating aspects of devotional practice that had waned in the meantime.

Gathering the threads

The mention of Canning Town brings to mind the time that David Sheppard – later Bishop of Liverpool – spent at the Mayflower Family Centre. In the 1960s the centre's aim was to create "an indigenous church with local leaders" from the white working class in the area. That didn't happen, but something far more unexpected did: the narrative turned global and the market in religion exploded.[25] But will it last? It isn't easy to say. Nor is it easy to answer the question posed at the beginning of this chapter concerning the exceptionality of London in British terms. In other words, is London a model that other cities may follow or is it an exceptional case?

> **Traditional readings of secularisation led us to assume a necessary incompatibility between religion and the urban environment.**

One point however is clear: the scope and diversity of the data demand a willingness to discover new ways of imagining the city. Traditional readings of secularisation led us to assume a necessary incompatibility between religion and the urban environment. Manifestly this is not the case and we need to understand why, both in London and elsewhere. This means looking at the abundance of new material with fresh eyes, allowing this to stimulate not only new ideas but new ways of speaking about the city (i.e. new forms of religious literacy) – both inside and outside the churches.

The shifting nature of national debates should be approached in a similar light.

1 Source: Census 2011, Office for National Statistics, licensed under the Open Government License v.2.0.

2 The marked difference between the Dioceses of London and Southwark requires careful reflection. At the very least, it resists easy generalisations about urban areas.

3 Bishop Richard Chartres, 'New Fire in London', Lambeth Lecture, 30 September 2015. See www.archbishopofcanterbury.org/articles.php/5621/bishop-of-london-delivers-lambeth-lecture-on-church-growth-in-the-capital

4 Peter Brierley, *Capital Growth: The London Church Census* (ADBC Publishers, 2013).

5 See issuu.com/londoncm/docs/london_church_census_2012_report

6 For more detail about the census results for London, see www.ons.gov.uk/ons/dcp29904_291554.pdf

7 Alan Piggot, *Stepney Episcopal Area Contextual Survey: Summary Report*, Diocese of London (November 2013). See www.thcofe.org/uploads/1/3/6/5/13654149/stepney_contextual_survey.pdf

8 Ibid., p. 5.

9 These church plants/mission initiatives operate under Bishops' Mission Orders; some are geographically based, others operate across more than one parish.

10 Bob Jackson and Alan Piggot, 'Another Capital Idea: Church Growth in the Diocese of London 2003-2010', an unpublished report for the Diocese of London, available at www.london.anglican.org/about/another-capital-idea/, p. 24.

11 Lois Lee, *Recognizing the Nonreligious* (OUP, 2016). In terms of the presence of non-religion in London itself, see also 'Godlessness in the global city', in David Garbin and Anna Strhan (eds), *Religion and the Global City* (Bloomsbury, 2017), pp. 135-52.

12 David Voas and Siobhan McAndrew, 'Three puzzles of non-religion in Britain', *Journal of Contemporary Religion*, 27 (1), 2012: 19-27.

13 For more information about this project, see www.birmingham.ac.uk/schools/ptr/departments/theologyandreligion/research/projects/megachurches/index.aspx. I am grateful for permission to quote from as yet unpublished material (see notes 14 and 16).

14 See Sophie Bremner, 'Black majority megachurches in London: Aspiring to engender change', Paper presented to the 'Megachurches and Social Engagement in London' Day Conference, 1 November 2016.

15 Alpha is an evangelistic course which seeks to introduce the basics of the Christian faith through a series of talks and discussions.

[16] See Sarah Dunlop, 'Anglican megachurches: Transforming society one person at a time', Paper presented to the 'Megachurches and Social Engagement in London' Day Conference, 1 November 2016, p. 6.

[17] See for example an interesting study of provision for the homeless: Paul Cloke, Sarah Johnsen and Jon May, 'Ethical citizenship? Faith-based volunteers and the ethics of providing services for homeless people', in Justin Beaumont and Paul Cloke (eds), *Faith-based Organisations and Exclusion in European Cities* (Policy Press, 2012), pp. 127-54.

[18] These debates are complex. See for example the material brought together in the projects on welfare referenced in Chapter 1 (p. 26). Interview data from these projects indicate that European populations are largely agreed that the state should be the principal provider of welfare. Such people are nonetheless realistic – well aware that European states are unable to fulfil these obligations to the required standard. In such circumstances it is better that the churches contribute what they can rather than nothing being done at all. For a summary article on this work, see Grace Davie, 'A European perspective on religion and welfare: Contrasts and commonalities', *Social Policy and Society*, 11 (4), 2012: 989–999.

[19] For a range of examples, see Grace Davie, *Religion in Britain*, pp. 137-40.

[20] For visitor numbers in 2016 see *www.alva.org.uk/details.cfm?p=423*. It is worth noting that visitor numbers stay high despite significant entry charges.

[21] For more information see *www.westminster-abbey.org/institute* and *www.stpaulsinstitute.org.uk/*

[22] See Grace Davie, *Religion in Britain*, pp. 38 and 83.

[23] See *rcdow.org.uk/news/annual-mass-for-migrants/*

[24] Alana Harris, 'Devout East Enders: Catholicism in the East End of London,' in David Goodhew (ed.), *Church Growth in Britain* (Ashgate, 2012), pp. 41-58.

[25] See Colin Marchant, 'The growth of new churches in Newham, 1980-2015', in David Goodhew and Anthony-Paul Cooper (eds) *No Secular City: Church Growth and Decline in London, 1980 to the Present* (Routledge, forthcoming).

3
National conversations:
whose feathers are ruffled?

The previous chapter closed with a brief reference to the work of Bishop David Sheppard at the Mayflower Centre in Canning Town. This one will begin with an account of **Faith in the City: A Call for Action by Church and Nation**, an initiative in which Bishop Sheppard played a crucial role.[1] The report was published in 1985. It will continue with a discussion of the controversy engendered by Salman Rushdie's **The Satanic Verses** which appeared three years later.[2] Between the two a significant change took place regarding the terms of debate, that is the turn to religion already noted in previous chapters. Here the significance of this shift for public discussion will be foregrounded as alignments alter and 'traditional' discourse is found wanting.

The final section places this shift in a global context noting three key dates: 1979, 1989 and 2001. The first marks the Iranian revolution – the moment when the Shah of Iran (a Western puppet) fled before an Ayatollah motivated by conservative readings of Islam. The second captures the fall of the Berlin Wall, the collapse of communism and all that followed from this. The third is 9/11 – an iconic moment in world politics. The question to ask at this stage is why no scholar, pundit or politician saw any of these events coming.

Faith in the City: context and controversy

The first of these dates (1979) marks a watershed in British politics. It was the moment when an evident lack of political will in the 1970s came to an abrupt end in the election of Margaret Thatcher as Prime Minister. No one, not even her worst enemies, could call Mrs Thatcher indecisive. Setting about her task with legendary determination, she introduced a series of political and economic initiatives with the specific aim of reversing what she perceived as Britain's calamitous national decline. Central to her thinking was a commitment to the market as the key to economic growth.

It is equally important to recall that in 1983 a left-leaning Labour Party experienced its worst electoral defeat since 1918, leaving a potentially dangerous void in political life. Who in this situation could speak on behalf of those who were caught at the sharp end of the far-reaching economic and social transformations advocated by the new government, and on what authority?

Into this situation stepped the churches, and notably the Church of England, which in 1985 produced *Faith in the City*. Much has been written about this document, which has become a touchstone for debate about the churches' role in public life. 'Presence', it is clear, was a hugely significant factor, specifically the capacities of a parochially-based church not only to reach, but to defend those parts of society – in this case neighbourhoods known as 'urban priority areas' (UPAs) – which were perceived as victims of economic change. Rubbished even before publication as 'pure Marxist theology', *Faith in the City* made its mark, reminding the nation as a whole that it could not simply forget the areas of society that were paying the price for economic regeneration. The state, the report declared, was as responsible for the inner cities of Britain as it was for its more leafy suburbs.

That was one interpretation of the facts. Unsurprisingly Mrs. Thatcher thought otherwise, drawing at least in part on her Methodist upbringing.[3] Self-improvement, she argued, was the responsibility of the individual, not of the state – a view strongly supported by a close friend, the then Chief Rabbi, Immanuel Jakobovits.[4] A fuller and even more explicit articulation of Mrs Thatcher's own position can be found in her address to the General Assembly of the Church of Scotland in May 1988. Known colloquially as the "Sermon on the Mound" this was effectively a theological justification of the market and laid great emphasis on the significance of individual choices. The assembled company – once again the representatives of a parochially organised national church – was not on the whole impressed. The moderator of the Church of Scotland responded to Mrs Thatcher's address by handing her recent reports from the churches on poverty, housing and a fair social benefit system. The gesture was interpreted as an implied rebuke.

Keeping both context and controversy in mind, it is worth looking in more detail at the content of *Faith in the City*. The report is divided into three sections. The first sets out the challenge of UPAs from various points of view: secular, ecclesiastical (i.e. the past and present role of the churches in city life) and theological. The second section speaks primarily to the Church – meaning the Church of England – and the third addresses the nation (in terms of urban policy, poverty, employment and work, housing, health, social care and community work, education and young people, and order and law). In all three sections, the references to diversity concern ethnic rather than religious (i.e. other-faith) communities. For example, the theological discussion includes three paragraphs (no more) on "The gospel and other faiths" – a passage that encourages a supportive rather than confrontational stance towards the non-Christian communities present in UPAs.[5] Conversely, there is considerable concern about both the absence of black minority groups in the Church's leadership and the relative disadvantage of ethnic minorities in secular life.

It is true that the chapter on education and young people goes a little further. Here, there is at least some awareness of the specific needs of Muslim families.[6] How might it be possible to promote forms of education that are sensitive to the faith and culture of diverse religious communities without exacerbating the tensions that endanger the cohesion of society as a whole? Paragraphs 13.55ff. develop this approach in terms of religious education and the adaptations that will be necessary to this subject in an increasingly pluralist society.

The 1988 Education Act is instructive in this respect. At this point, the growing presence of other faiths was clearly acknowledged, but in a rather backhanded fashion. In its early drafts, religious education occupied but a few lines of the Bill; it looked as though it could end by being more than ever a Cinderella subject. The Bill, however, provoked vigorous protests, led for the most part by lay politicians, notably Baroness Cox and a group of supporters in the House of Lords. Discussions with the Secretary of State followed, mediated by the Bishop of London. In the final draft of the Act the clauses on religious education occupied fifteen pages, including an explicit reference to the Christian content of religious teaching.[7] Such an emphasis partly reflected the growing trend towards comparative religion in the classroom, but at the same time demonstrated – conclusively – that Christianity could no longer be taken for granted as the only world faith present in modern Britain. It had rather to be affirmed. Provision was made for schools with a significant number of children from other-faith families, but only by contracting out of the (Christian) norm.

The adequacy of these arrangements for the current (i.e. 21st century) context has been sharply called into question. Such concerns are well summarised in the material relating to the Commission on RE, established in 2016 by the Religious Education Council. The Commission will report in 2018.[8]

Retrospective accounts

Faith in the City was a landmark report regarding the relationship between Church and state. The following events capture not only its content but its longer-term consequences. The first took the form of a 'witness seminar' held at the Institute for Historical Research in July 2006. Such seminars – a model developed by the Institute for Contemporary British History – are a specialised form of oral history in which a range people associated with a particular event are brought together to discuss, debate, and even disagree about their recollections. The 2006 seminar was organised by Eliza Philby (the author of *God and Mrs Thatcher*) and chaired by Hugh McLeod, a distinguished historian of religion.[9] Much of the discussion concerned the context, origins and process of *Faith in the City*. Particularly significant in my view were the reflections pertaining to the willingness of distinguished individuals to serve on the Commission, not least its Chair (Sir Richard O'Brien), seeing this – an initiative of the established Church – as a way to draw attention to the plight of communities in both the inner cities and outer estates of Britain's larger conurbations. Significant sections of the population were suffering the effects of economic exclusion at a moment when the Labour Party (the natural outlet for such feelings) was effectively side-lined.

Some ten years later, in January 2016, the Cabinet papers referring to *Faith in the City* were released under the 30 years rule, provoking further discussion of the report and the subsequent controversy. There is no lack of evidence in these papers for the acrimonious exchanges that took place at the time. The accusations of 'pure Marxist theology' were not only real but heartfelt. In its coverage of this episode, The *Church Times* recalled its leader in the week of the Report's publication, which read:

> *This Archbishop's Commission has done a major and radical job in bringing together the best insights of pastors and evangelists who have been pondering the challenge of Britain's new ghettos. What they have to say may often seem disturbing to a Church which is predominantly middle class, still substantially rural and almost entirely white. But already the Church of England has done something for these areas; at least it has not withdrawn from them.[10]*

Much has changed since that paragraph was written, not least the influx of global Christians and the rebalancing of urban and rural in church life. Most important of all, however, is the continuing awareness that a parochially-based church is able to reach sections of society that other organisations (religious or secular) cannot.

The third event is a little different and concerns the companion volume to *Faith in the City*. *Faith in the Countryside* (published in 1990) was both similar to and different from the earlier report.[11] It was similar in that it operated in more or less the same way and reported to both Church and nation, but different in its political colour (one-nation Tory rather than left of centre) and markedly less controversial. Its content, moreover, began to reflect issues pertaining to the 1990s rather than the 1980s – notably a growing preoccupation with environmental concerns and a greater awareness of the European dimension. Justice and peace issues (that familiar duo) were no longer separable from 'the integrity of creation' and all three increasingly transcended national boundaries.

The Satanic Verses and its aftermath

More immediately, we need to address what became known as 'the Rushdie affair'.[12] The bare bones of the story can be summarised as follows. In 1988, Salman Rushdie published *The Satanic Verses*, a novel deemed blasphemous by Muslims, whose initial and understandable outrage led eventually to public book burnings. In February 1989, the Ayatollah Khomeini (of Iran) proclaimed a *fatwa* declaring the author guilty of blasphemy and Rushdie was forced into hiding. In December 1990, Rushdie publicly embraced Islam – a key moment in the chain of events but one that was not reciprocated by the religious authorities in Iran who re-affirmed the *fatwa*. Lives were lost in violent encounters outside Britain, including the stabbing to death of the translator of the Japanese edition. In short, this was an episode that challenged almost every assumption of a modern, liberal and supposedly tolerant society. The fact that Rushdie was himself of Indian and Islamic origin simply made the sequence of events more complex.

It is the intractability of the underlying issues that requires attention. At stake were the relative merits of two 'freedoms': freedom of religion on the one hand and freedom of speech on the other. The Muslim community invoked the former (faith should be inviolate – i.e. free from insult), whilst Salman Rushdie and his supporters were claiming the latter (the right to publish freely). Pushed to extremes, the two collided – a situation that has recurred all over Europe (see below). Specific to the British controversy, however, was the moment in 1990 already indicated. With every appearance of sincerity, Rushdie declared himself a Muslim, apologising to his co-religionists for the problems caused by the book and acknowledging that some passages were offensive to believers.

In effect this was an admission of blasphemy. Financial contributions from the book's royalties would be made to those who had suffered injury as a result of the protests. Rushdie's attempt to build bridges seemed genuine enough and brought some comfort to the Muslim community. The respite, however, was short lived and the subsequent retraction (a second insult) hard to take.

Just as troubling was the genuine incomprehension of the British public, who had great difficulty grasping the hurt of the Muslim community. Quite simply, the religious sensibilities of most British people were of a different order. Assuming a live-and-let-live approach to religious issues, it was hard to understand why the publication of a book caused so much anger when no one was obliged to read it in the first place. Part of being British, it seemed, was to accept a low-key approach to religion, with the strong implication that anyone who comes to live in these islands – for whatever reason – should conform, in public at least, to a similar view. But does this essentially conditional statement provide an adequate basis for a truly tolerant and pluralist society? The vehemence of the ensuing controversy suggests that it does not.

Hence the centrality of the Rushdie affair to the argument presented here. It marks the moment when ethnicity as a category ceded the place to religion, a shift of particular importance for Muslims – a relatively disparate population in terms of ethnicity who were instinctively drawn together at this point. Paradoxically the controversy had the opposite effect on liberal opinion. Those who were united in their support for ethnic or national minorities were much less at ease when it came to religious issues. Different points of view emerged in a debate that found its focus in the competing freedoms outlined above. For the majority, freedom of speech was paramount; for others (considerably fewer) this was tempered by empathy for the Muslim minority.

Unsurprisingly, a cascade of publications followed. Paul Weller's *A Mirror for our Times: 'The Rushdie Affair' and the Future of Multiculturalism* is an essential guide in this respect.[13] Published on the 20th anniversary of the initial controversy, the book constitutes an admirably balanced account of the episode itself, its aftermath, its effects on policy and policy-makers and the secondary literature it has generated.

Weller begins by reconstructing the sequence of events following publication. Drawing on a huge range of resources,[14] he establishes a narrative that is noticeably more nuanced than that depicted by the media. The steps by which a primarily literary event became the trigger for a global crisis are not self-evident; each one of them needs careful explanation. The time-line however is simply the starting point. The chapters that follow reflect on broader issues: the nature of Islam, its place in British and European society and the implications for policy-making. The idea of "a mirror for our times" frames this analysis; it is taken from the reflections of Bhikku Parekh – a prominent political scientist and a former chair of the Commission for Racial Equality. As early as 1989, Parekh saw in the Rushdie crisis a mirror that not only reflects but magnifies the underlying trends in British society. For this reason alone, it merits maximum scrutiny. In terms of policy, the key concept is 'multiculturalism', meaning by this an attempt not only to create but to sustain a society that is at ease with its own diversity. Already controversial, the idea has become more so in subsequent decades.

European equivalents

This is not solely a British story. Equivalents occurred in relatively quick succession right across Europe. A by no means exhaustive list would include controversies about the Muslim headscarf *(l'affaire du foulard)* in France, which also began in 1989; the murder of Theo van Gogh (2004) in The Netherlands, together with the subsequent defection of Hirsi Ali to the United States; the furore over the cartoons of Mohammed published by a Danish newspaper (in 2005), a debate that subsequently spread to Sweden (2007); the challenge to the legality of minarets in a Swiss referendum (2009); and more recently the banning of the *burqa* or *niqab* in public places in some, if not all, European countries.

Each one of these cases captures something of the country in question as well as the place of religion and religious minorities in this. Key in this respect is an appreciation that the secularisation process has taken place differently in different European nations.[15] For example, what in Britain, and indeed in most of northern Europe, occurred gradually (starting with a de-clericalisation of the churches from within at the time of the Reformation), became in France a delayed and much more ideological clash between a hegemonic, heavily clerical church and a much more militant secular state. The result was 'la guerre des deux Frances' (Catholic and *laïque*), which dominated French political life well into the 20th century. The legacies still remain in the form of a self-consciously secular elite, and a lingering suspicion concerning religion of all kinds. *Laïcité* becomes the key concept. Understood as the absence of religion in the public sphere, it accounts for the acuteness of French anxieties regarding visible symbols of religion in public life (not least the school system).

Britain has evolved differently and broadly speaking is less democratic than France, both constitutionally and institutionally, but more tolerant. Visible symbols of religion are by and large acceptable in public life. Think, for example, of passport control at Heathrow, where not only headscarves but turbans are almost always in evidence, something unthinkable at Charles de Gaulle. But in Britain too can be found some sharply secular voices, as evidenced by the Rushdie controversy itself. The French, conversely, were somewhat bewildered by a debate concerning blasphemy (and blasphemy law) in a neighbouring society in the late 20th century.

That said, the clash between freedom of speech and freedom of religion erupted dramatically in France in the form of terrorist attacks on the premises of *Charlie Hebdo* – a well-known satirical magazine. The first took place in 2011 and the second in 2015.[16] Both were provoked by controversial depictions of Mohammed. In 2011, the offices of the magazine were burnt out; in 2015, the consequences were devastating and claimed the lives of twelve people including the director of *Charlie Hebdo* and several prominent cartoonists. Controversy raged once again. Seen by many as an accident waiting to happen, the incident raises very similar issues to the Rushdie controversy; among them moral as well as legal questions. No satirist deserves to die (none of us would dream of saying otherwise), but was it wise to flaunt quite so flagrantly the legal right to offend, whilst setting aside the moral duty not to? Such a stance is dangerous. As Nigel Biggar reminds us, the right to freedom of speech is precious. Specifically, "[i]t lets us criticise what's customary and conventional and established, be they beliefs or practices or institutions. It makes possible the seeds of revision, reform and progress. It enables individuals and societies and polities to learn, perhaps to change for the better".[17] Is it wise, therefore, to act in a way that jeopardises that freedom, and to run the risk of damaging (sometimes beyond repair) the consensus on which it depends?

Lessons learnt?

With this in mind, the following – somewhat depressing – question cannot be avoided: have we learnt nothing in the last two and half decades? The *Charlie Hebdo* outburst is, it seems, simply one more example of an ill-informed and ill-mannered debate about religion in public life, which raises issues of extreme importance to the democratic future of the countries in question, but remains sadly lacking in answers.

One shift, however, is clear: a significant adjustment has slowly but surely taken place, neatly captured in the ways that different groups of people react to religious controversy. In the 1980s, the discussion was largely about socio-economic issues and centred on the negative consequences of an over-rigorous application of monetarist policies. The 'attack' was directed at the New Right, some of whom reacted sharply to what was considered an unwarranted intrusion by churches and church people in political affairs. Those on the political left, though largely side-lined from political activity and not always sympathetic to the churches, were unlikely to object. A generation or so later, things are different. Religious controversy continues but for different reasons. In the main, it concerns the competing rights of secular and religious constituencies, recognising

Those whose political predilections led them to defend minority groups disadvantaged by racial or ethnic factors are much less likely to defend the religious aspirations of the self-same people.

that the latter are not only much more varied, but are more ready to press their claims in public as well as private life. The ruffled feathers are found this time amongst increasingly self-conscious secularists, often – but by no means only – on the political left. An important reason for this shift can be found in a point already made: it concerns the evolving constructions of the minorities currently present in Britain (and indeed elsewhere). Those whose political predilections led them to defend minority groups disadvantaged by racial or ethnic factors are much less likely to defend the religious aspirations of the self-same people.

Two rather different points conclude this discussion. First, it is worth noting that disproportionate numbers of journalists feel similar discomfort in this respect – unsurprisingly, perhaps, in that media personnel (as a profession) profess lower levels of religious commitment than the population as a whole, and have difficulty comprehending the issues at stake.[18] There are some notable exceptions, but on the whole national coverage of religion is poor and lacks the correctives that come from local knowledge (as alluded to in Chapter 1). And second and more far-reaching: is this the moment when class-based allegiances begin to give way to something closer to identity? In other words, does the shift described in the previous paragraph prefigure the voting patterns that in 2016 defied expectations on both sides of the Atlantic?

Religion in the modern world

The questions that follow are complex, compounded by the visibility of religion in the modern world – a factor in its own right. As indicated at the start of this chapter, the renewed awareness of religion will be approached with reference to key dates; it will start by paying attention to a cluster of changes taking place in 1979.

The dramatic shift in the political climate in Britain has already been foregrounded, not least Mrs Thatcher's unswerving commitment to the market as the key to economic growth. It was this conviction, moreover, that she shared with Ronald Reagan, with the effect that the 1980s constituted a decade in which the 'special relationship' between Britain and the United States developed in new ways. There was no equivalent to Mrs. Thatcher in continental Europe which resisted for longer the rolling back of the state.

A book that not only captures these shifts, but relates them to equally important developments elsewhere was published in the spring of 2013.[19] Christian Caryl's text weaves together a complex narrative which involves four protagonists and five countries. The protagonists are Mrs. Thatcher, Deng Xiaoping, the Ayatollah Khomeini and Pope John Paul II. The five countries are the United Kingdom, China, Iran, its neighbour Afghanistan, and Poland, then part of the Eastern bloc. Mrs. Thatcher and Deng initiated market reforms challenging deeply held assumptions about the way to manage the economy. The Ayatollah and John Paul II, conversely, were motivated by their respective religions to challenge the secular state. In Afghanistan, Islamism became a major factor in the resistance to the Soviet Union, as did Catholicism in Poland.

The imaginative leap in Caryl's analysis is to draw these factors together:

> *The forces unleashed in 1979 marked the beginning of the end of the great socialist utopia that had dominated so much of the 20th century. These five stories – the Iranian Revolution, the start of the Afghan jihad, Thatcher's election victory, the pope's first*

> Polish pilgrimage, and the launch of China's economic reforms
> – deflected the course of history in a radically new direction.
> It was in 1979 that the twin forces of the markets and religion,
> discounted for so long, came back with a vengeance.[20]

The 'victims' in this particular scenario were the dominant ideologies of the 20th century embodied in the secular state, in its socialist or communist forms. Both adjective (secular) and noun (state) are important in a formulation which was seen as the lynch pin of modernisation. To be modern meant to be secular and the accepted form of political organisation was the state. The 'new' combination of market and religion not only erodes both elements but reveals the connections between 1979 and 1989, and in the fullness of time 2001. By 1989, the market had proved itself more effective than the command economy of the Soviet Union, and religion – whether Muslim or Christian – was clearly more durable than its secular equivalent, in this case Communism. Forces set in train in 1979 led inexorably to the fall of the Berlin wall just over ten years later, and the collapse of the Soviet Union overall led in turn to a radical realignment of the global order which – to an extent – is still in train. The attack on the Twin Towers in 2001 is not covered in Caryl's account but the connections are clear enough. Quite clearly Islamism is one factor among others behind this epochal moment, to the evident bewilderment of the West.

> **To be modern meant to be secular and the accepted form of political organisation was the state.**

It is important to remember that Caryl is writing some thirty years after the event and can make connections that were not at all clear at the time. Indeed for those involved the principal feature that linked these three world-changing events was their unexpectedness. Manifestly, both policy-makers and pundits were caught unawares – in every case. Why was it that the Shah of Iran, a western figurehead, was obliged to flee before an Ayatollah motivated by conservative readings of Islam? And why did observers of all kinds fail to anticipate the concatenation of events that led to the fall of the Berlin wall and the collapse of communism as a credible narrative? And why finally did the events of 9/11 come like a bolt from the blue? By this stage there was a growing awareness of events in the Muslim world and their significance for Western policy,[21] but nobody – nobody at all – expected hijacked planes to fly into iconic

Was it really the case that religion (or God) was back?

buildings in New York. Hence the abruptness of the wake-up call: religion was undeniably important in that it was clearly able to motivate widely different groups of people to act in dramatic and unforeseen ways – a realisation that prompted renewed attention to an aspect of society that had been ignored for too long.

The wrong inference was drawn, however. All too quickly commentators began to assume that religion was resurgent or back, reasoning that we are now in a post-secular, rather than a post-religious, situation. To argue thus, however, is to conflate two rather different things. Was it really the case that religion (or God) was back?[22] Or was it simply that the disciplines of social science in the west, along with a wide variety of policy-makers, had now become aware (or re-aware) of something that had been there all the time? Was it, in other words, perceptions that had altered rather than reality? It is, I think, a complex mixture of both. New forms of religion have asserted themselves in different parts of the world; that is beyond doubt. It is incorrect to assume, however, that the new manifestations emerged from a vacuum. In almost all global regions, the presence of religion has been not only continuous but taken for granted; only in Europe might this statement be questioned, and then only partially.

It is against this background that we can engage the questions set out in the following chapter – drawn from material relating to the International Panel on Social Progress (IPSP) and the place of religion in this. What is the relationship between religion and social progress? And how can social science contribute to a better understanding of this question?

[1] This was the report of the Archbishop of Canterbury's Commission on Urban Priority Areas (Church House Publishing, 1985).

[2] Salman Rushdie, *The Satanic Verses* (Viking-Penguin, 1988).

[3] The links between Mrs Thatcher's religious views and her political policies are explored in detail in Eliza Filby, *God and Mrs Thatcher: Conviction Politics in Britain's Secular Age* (Biteback Publishing, 2015).

[4] Arguing thus, Lord Jacobovits controversially recalled the capacities of individual Jewish immigrants to work their way out of poverty; he expected those more recently arrived to do the same regardless of their background – a view that directly challenged *Faith in the City*, which recognised the plight of ethnic minorities as a whole.

[5] *Faith in the City*, pp. 60-1.

[6] *Faith in the City*, pp. 302 ff.

[7] Specifically an agreed syllabus "shall reflect the fact that the religious traditions in Great Britain are in the main Christian whilst taking account of the teaching and practices of the other principal religions represented in Great Britain", (Education Reform Act 1988, chapter 40, clause 1, section 8.3).

[8] More information on this important work can be found on: *www.commissiononre.org.uk/about-the-commission-on-religious-education/*. An interim report was published in September 2017. See *www.commissiononre.org.uk/religious-education-for-all-commission-interim-report*

[9] For more detail see *www.timeshighereducation.co.uk/story.asp?storyCode=204583&sectioncode=26*

[10] *Church Times*, Leader, 6 December 1985, p. 9.

[11] 'The Report of the Archbishops' Commission on Rural Areas' (Church House Publishing, 1985).

[12] See Paul Weller, *A Mirror for our Times: The Rushdie Affair and the Future of Multiculturalism* (Continuum, 2009), who notes (p. 2) that many Muslims prefer not to use the term 'Rushdie affair' given that it points to the author rather than the book. For this constituency 'the *Satanic Verses* controversy' is a more accurate description.

[13] See note 12.

[14] See, for example, the extensive reference list in the opening pages of Weller's account and its meticulously ordered bibliography.

[15] See David Martin, *A General Theory of Secularization* (Blackwell 1978).

[16] A good collection of material on the *Charlie Hebdo* 'story' can be found at *www.theguardian.com/media/charlie-hebdo*

[17] Nigel Biggar, 'Charlie Hebdo took offensiveness too far', *The Times,* 9 January 2016.

[18] Neil Thurman, Alessio Cornia and Jessica Kunert, *Journalists in the UK* (Reuters Institute for the Study of Journalism, 2016), especially pp. 10-11.

[19] Christian Caryl, *Strange Rebels: 1979 and the Birth of the 21st Century* (Basic Books, 2013). Paradoxically, publication coincided almost exactly with Baroness Thatcher's death – a moment when her political philosophy was revisited in some detail.

[20] Ibid., p. xiii.

[21] Samuel Huntington's *The Clash of Civilizations: The Remaking of the World Order* (Simon and Schuster, 2013) can be taken as an example. His thinking on the clash of civilisations dominated debate in the 1990s, both in the United States and beyond.

[22] The shorthand of 'God is Back' is taken from the title of a widely read book; see John Micklethwait and Adrian Wooldridge, *God is Back: How the Global Rise of Faith is Changing the World* (Penguin 2010).

4
Global challenges: the contributions of social science

This chapter is a little different. It examines a global initiative of which I was part: the International Panel on Social Progress (IPSP). The sections that follow start by outlining the project itself before addressing the material on religion within this and the questions that ensue. The final section expands one issue in more detail, that is the role of religious thinking in the increasingly urgent debate about climate change. It pays close attention to **Laudato si'**, the 2015 papal encyclical entitled "On Care for Our Common Home",[1] and its reception amongst a wide variety of audiences.

The International Panel on Social Progress

The International Panel on Social Progress brought together more than three hundred scholars, from a wide range of disciplines and from many different parts of the world, to assess and synthesise the state-of-the-art knowledge that bears on social progress across a wide range of economic, political and cultural questions.[2] The goal was to provide the target audience (individuals, movements, organisations, politicians, decision-makers and practitioners) with the best expertise that social science can offer.

The process – to a significant extent modelled on the Intercontinental Panel on Climate Change (IPCC) – has been a long one. A team of five to ten authors took responsibility for each of the 22 chapters, working under the direction of two co-ordinating lead authors. Following IPCC practice, an initial draft of the chapters was posted on line for several months in the latter part of 2016 in order to collect comments from the widest possible audience and to allow the authors to read and respond to each other's work. A second draft was prepared with the comments in mind. The report as a whole will be published in 2018; there will also be a summary version for a more general audience.[3]

There are two introductory and two concluding chapters in the full report. The remaining eighteen are divided into three sections: economic, political and cultural. Unsurprisingly the chapter on religion – entitled "Religions and social progress: Critical assessments and creative partnerships" – falls into the last of these categories, along with the material on cultural change, the pluralisation of families, global health and the parameters of human living, education, and belonging and solidarity. Social progress – the key to the whole enterprise – is defined in Chapter 2.

Setting aside Enlightenment assumptions that progress is somehow built into history, the chapter constructs what its authors take to be the most important normative dimensions for making comparisons in this multifaceted arena (over time and between places). These are conceptualised as values (against which to measure progress) and principles (which guide action). The notion of a compass is deployed as a metaphor in the sense that it sets the line of travel, recognising that the map in question is complex and the destination elusive. What is considered progress in one situation may be differently assessed in another.

The chapter on religion

At more or less the same time as I agreed to give the 2016 Cadbury Lectures, I was invited to become a Co-ordinating Lead Author (CLA) for the chapter on religion in the IPSP report. Thus the two activities ran side by side and each encouraged the other. The IPSP process required two CLAs (from different parts of the world) to work alongside each other in each chapter team. I was not only delighted, but honoured, when

Nancy Ammerman (a distinguished sociologist of religion from Boston University) agreed to join me in this task.

The first step was to build the team, bearing in mind that we needed expertise from different disciplines, different world faiths and different global regions in order to cover the literature. Above all, we needed hands-on experience in empirical work, in order that our text might be fully grounded in the realities of religion as they exist in different parts of the world. At the same time we had to find a discourse – a literacy – that related these realities to the concept of social progress as this was understood by the project as a whole. We had, finally, to find ways of making this speak to a diverse readership both inside and outside the academy. Every member of the team contributed to this task.

> **Religion is a lived, situated and constantly changing reality, and has as much to do with navigating everyday life as it does with the supernatural.**

Defining the task and defining religion

The first meeting of the IPSP authors (including ourselves) took place in Istanbul in August 2015. It was a learning experience in every sense of the term. Not only was this the first time that the chapter team had come together (some of them travelling many thousands of miles), it was also the moment when we appreciated that significant sections of the social-scientific community were hesitant about the relationship between religion and social progress as we were learning to understand this. This hesitancy took two forms: either religion was considered irrelevant (i.e. no longer of significance), or it was negatively perceived – in other words inimical to social progress. The fact that religion was (or more accurately was deemed to be) 'back' was therefore a problem.

In the 48 hours that we spent together, we worked hard on finding ways to counter these at best partial, and at worst inaccurate, views starting with a clear definition of religion itself. Escaping the limitations of a purely Western perspective was the first step. We argue that religion is more – much more – than the broad range of institutions and beliefs traditionally recognised by social science; it is rather a very much larger cultural domain that encompasses the beliefs and practice of the vast majority (over 80%) of the world's population.[4] Religion is a lived, situated and constantly changing reality, and has as much to do with navigating everyday life as it does with the supernatural. It follows that secularity should be considered an equally fluid entity, whose distinction from religion will vary from place to place – a division decided more by the context in question that by pre-determined categories. That said, we recognise that what we term humanity's 'limiting conditions' – death, suffering, injustice – are likely to be confronted and explained in religious terms across a wide range of societies.

From this starting point we developed our approach to the relationship between religion and social progress. Our task was to scour the available literature in order to document our case, but we began from the belief that neither good nor ill could be assumed from the outset. We had rather to look case-by-case in different social and cultural domains, and in different parts of the world, to see what was happening on the ground. We were well aware that particular forms of religion were perceived negatively, sometimes rightly so. Without doubt religion can take forms that are destructive of people and places. Elsewhere, however, religious individuals and religious communities are manifestly associated with the health and wellbeing of their respective societies – an entirely positive feature.

Expanding the field

In order to get a grip on the agenda, we worked 'upwards' from the micro to the macro (a little like the chapters in this essay). Specifically we began with the most intimate of human relationships (i.e. those that relate to gender, sexuality and the family), appreciating that these have been moulded from time immemorial by religious rules, rituals, and prohibitions. But here as elsewhere, it is important to set aside an over-simple binary between secular progress and religious reaction – the reality is infinitely more complex. The focus on everyday lived religion was a valuable corrective in this respect. It pointed us to a multi-disciplinary literature that documents the ways in which men, women and young people negotiate their very personal lives. It is clear that they accept some of the limitations that derive from religion but question others, and extract from these complex negotiations the means to confront the vicissitudes of life.

For example, certain forms of conservative religion undoubtedly resist progress, notably when 'fundamentalist' types of religion challenge (at times violently) what they deem to be the sexual 'decadence' associated with the West. Less well known are the subtle ways in which (mostly) women deploy or even subvert their religiously-ascribed roles to construct fulfilling lives for both themselves and their families. Yet other women advance their cause in religiously-based reform movements or alternative spiritualities, rather than – or as well as – secular substitutes. It is important, finally, to recall that the divisions between conservative and more liberal approaches run through the world's religions rather than between them – a theme that pervades our chapter.

The subsequent sections deal with political issues. The first addresses the question of diversity – looking (a) at its shape and forms in the late modern world and (b) at its governance. A constructive starting point lies in the recognition that *religious* diversity is part and parcel of a broader agenda, but that it has particular characteristics. Religious differences, for example, are likely to raise more intractable questions than variations in taste or style. Equally central is an awareness that diversities exist, largely (if not exclusively) because of the movement of people, both forced and unforced. An overall increase in religious diversity should not however be assumed. In some global regions (the modern Middle East for instance) it declines as religious minorities are forced to leave; in others it grows as significant numbers of migrants arrive (West Europe); and in yet other parts of the world it has been there for centuries (S.E. Asia). Whatever the case, it is important to note the two-way flows between religion and migration. On the one hand, religions inspire, manage and benefit from the migration process but on the other, they are shaped and moulded by the dislocations of populations that inevitably ensue. You cannot have one without the other.

The consequences require careful management: migration is a hot political issue. For this reason, we reflect carefully on the various forms of governance discovered in this field and the debates that surround them. These include the pros and cons of multiculturalism, of diverse forms of secularism, and of democracy itself. We recognise, however, that there are deeper questions to address: those that probe the ways in which religiously diverse people do not simply co-exist, but flourish in each other's company. We discover, for example, that 'street level ecumenism' (working side by side) is often more effective than a dialogue between elites.[5] Such an approach drives us back once again to the realities of lived religion in addition to its official formulations.

The second of our political sections confronts directly the much talked-of connections between religion and conflict. The core argument is easily stated. To ask whether religion – or certain forms of religion – causes conflict or violence is not the most helpful approach. Much more constructive are enquiries that look systematically at the circumstances in which a violent outcome is likely. Contestation over physical spaces is one such, as is an excess of regulation which leads all too often to negative attitudes towards minorities. Even more important is the considerable evidence that weak or failed states (and the fragile economies associated with them) encourage – by default – violent and authoritarian attempts to restore order. Some of these are religiously inspired.

There is, however, another side to this coin. Clearly there are situations in which religion becomes entangled with violence, but it is equally a resource for peace-making. This can be seen in the attention to values (those associated with justice or righteousness) promulgated by all the world faiths; it can also be expressed organisationally. Both dimensions are illustrated in the local and concrete – in, for example, the sensitive management of particular sacred spaces – and in the deep expertise of global movements such as the Sant'Egidio Community, the World Council of Churches and (to give but one American example) the Interfaith Dialogue and Peacebuilding Program at the US Institute of Peace. It is equally clear that religious actors are often critical players in post-conflict situations: good examples can be found in South Africa or Northern Ireland.

The relationship between religion and human rights offers a linking theme in this respect. The concept of human rights has become a defining discourse in the management of diversity, in the resolution of conflict and in the fair distribution of resources. Across all of these domains, however, the relationship between religion and human rights is differently regarded: from active advocacy at one end of the spectrum to open hostility at the other. There are those who draw from Article 18 of the United Nations Declaration on Human Rights to uphold the freedom of religion and belief as a fundamental and universally applicable human right; there are others who see the demands of religion and religious people as inimical to an alternative range of freedoms (those, for instance, of free speech, of women and of LGBTi communities). The existence of a UN Special Rapporteur on Freedom of Religion and Belief is indicative of a determination to find a way forward not only in places where diverse religious and secular norms are valued, but also in places where they are likely to come into conflict – gender-specific abuses being a case in point.

There are two further substantive sections in the IPSP chapter. The first picks up a theme that runs right through this essay in that it deals with the place of religion in the wellbeing of individuals and communities. Particular attention is paid to welfare, education and healthcare. A striking example will be taken to illustrate the approach. Faced with the seeming impasse between secular health professionals and faith-based initiatives in parts of the developing world, a series of contributions in *The Lancet* offers an evidence-based way forward.[6] The emphasis is on partnership, arguing that secular and faith-based organisations can work together even when there are areas of disagreement regarding policy and practice.

The crucial point is to ascertain exactly what these are – and thus to establish not only what cannot be done in partnership but the (normally much greater) areas of work that can be shared. The need is such that it is unwise to rule out significant resources on principle. Not all partnerships with religious organisations are advisable but many are – a theme to be pursued shortly.

Before doing so, one further area requires attention – that is the role of faith-based organisations in caring for the earth itself (the final step in our ascending scale). Unsurprisingly, given its genesis, a number of chapters in the IPSP report engage growing concerns about the environment and the role of social science – as well as natural science – in understanding these better. Our task was more specific: namely to draw attention to the place of religious groups in this enterprise. Again a single example captures the potential. *Laudato si'* – the second encyclical of Pope Francis – was published in 2015; it has become a defining moment in the debate about climate change. Its content and significance will be developed in the final section of this chapter.

More immediately, the concluding paragraphs of our IPSP chapter took the form of an action toolkit, which found its rationale in a set of cross-cutting themes that ran right through our material. These include the persistence of religion in the modern world; the importance of context in discerning outcomes (both positive and negative); the urgent need to enhance cultural competence (not least religious literacy) in different parts of the world; the significance of religion in initiating change; and the gains that accrue from effective partnerships. Not all of these can be pursued here, but the following stand out. First is the continuing need for assessment and – where necessary – constructive criticism, bearing in mind that social progress not only evolves but looks different in different places. Second are the demonstrable benefits of well-judged partnerships, noting that 'well-judged' is the crucial word in this sentence. As my colleague Nancy Ammerman has put this:

> *researchers and policy-makers pursuing social progress will benefit from careful attention to the power of religious ideas to motivate, of religious practices to shape ways of life, of religious communities to mobilize and extend the reach of social changes, and of religious leaders and symbols to legitimate call to action.*[7]

She is right.

Laudato si' – a step change in global debate

Pope Francis' second encyclical, *Laudato si'*, offers an excellent illustration of all four of these features.[8] It has, moreover, brought about a step change in the debate surrounding climate change. It is not difficult to see why. It is not only the size of the Pope's constituency that counts (though that most certainly matters), but the fact that the encyclical draws on established scientific research to deliver a powerful *ethical* message: that deprived communities will suffer most from the changes taking place. Taking both these points together, there can be no doubt that the Pope has vastly extended not only the reach but the impact of the debate – a fact recognised as much by scientists as by theologians.

An opinion piece in *The Guardian* puts it thus:

> *Pope Francis's encyclical on climate change,* Laudato si', *is the most astonishing and perhaps the most ambitious papal document of the past 100 years, since it is addressed not just to Catholics, or Christians, but to everyone on earth.*[9]

The following sentence goes further still: it argues that the encyclical sets out a programme for change that is rooted in human needs but makes "the radical claim that these needs are not primarily greedy and selfish ones." Rather we need nature just as we need each other. Thus the care for nature and the care for the poor are two sides of the same coin. The environment, in the Pope's understanding of the term, captures the underlying connectedness of the world and all those who inhabit it. It is this relationship – the indissoluble link between nature and human beings – that lies at the heart of the document.

Equally striking is the editorial in *Nature*, a prestigious and widely-cited scientific journal. The encyclical is warmly commended for the accuracy of the science. But even more arresting is the awareness that the moral authority and popularity of the Pope will ensure a readership that scientific papers can only dream of; the Catholic Church, moreover, "has a superb means of spreading the word every Sunday".[10] This is not the phraseology that one expects from a scientific journal of this standing.

The final paragraph of the Introduction to *Laudato si'* articulates the key themes of the encyclical itself – those that appear and reappear in each chapter as the overall message unfolds. Relationship and interconnectedness head the list and underpin the subsequent critique. Central to the latter is the impossibility of a technological fix to the problems that we face and the need for new – radically new – ways of thinking. The recurring themes are:

> ...the intimate relationship between the poor and the
> fragility of the planet, the conviction that everything in the
> world is connected, the critique of new paradigms and forms

*of power derived from technology, the call to seek other ways
of understanding the economy and progress, the value proper
to each creature, the human meaning of ecology, the need
for forthright and honest debate, the serious responsibility of
international and local policy, the throwaway culture and the
proposal of a new lifestyle. (§16)*

The list reflects a serious indictment of current practice alongside a powerful affirmation of alternative values.

The encyclical generated huge media interest and a significant secondary literature. The necessarily selective discussion that follows draws from an inter-disciplinary set of articles, collected under the title: "The Pope's Fateful Vision of Hope for Society and the Planet".[11] This includes an editorial and five responses which reflect on the encyclical from a social-scientific perspective. It becomes in effect a three-way conversation in which a cluster of social scientists interrogate the relationship between religion, science and social science. A range of opinions emerge.

In their editorial statement, Brulle and Antonio suggest that *Laudato si'* offers a model – an exemplar even – for inter-disciplinary work applied to a common problem; it has opened the debate between science and religion in new ways. The argument is pursued in the first commentary piece. Here the same authors applaud the Pope's initiative in bringing a moral vision to a scientific problem, recognising the power of narrative to galvanise effective action. Deploying their knowledge of social science, they demonstrate the link between discursive 'framing' and the success (or otherwise) of a social movement. The comparison between Pope Francis and Martin Luther King catches the eye.

Erik Olin Wright is not so sure. He recognises that the encyclical "provides a powerful indictment of the social practices that have contributed to environmental and social degradation", and that it contains "a passionate call for radical transformation of our relationship to nature". That, however, is not enough. Missing is an informed discussion about how these ideas will be translated into effective action. It will take more than good will to overturn the structural imbalances of the capitalist system in either its economic or political forms. Erlich and Harte raise a different, but equally penetrating point, that is the failure of Pope Francis to tackle the demographic questions associated with climate change (a lacuna also noted in the *Nature* editorial). The argument turns on Pope Francis' claim that that "demographic growth is fully compatible with an integral and shared development" (§50). Erlich and Harte disagree. Demographic trends are as much part of the problem as rampant consumerism: indeed each compounds the other as a driver of environmental degradation.

The two final commentaries return to the positive. Both, moreover, recognise the significance of connecting the scientific discussion of climate change to wider social processes. Anabela Carvalho emphasises the consequent democratisation of the central issues. She strongly endorses the Pope's call for a fully democratic and inclusive conversation at every level of society; in this sense the encyclical is a highly effective appeal to greater citizen engagement. Finally Edenhofer, Flachsland and Knopf remind us that much about *Laudato si'* is indeed unprecedented – not only its boldness in addressing the entire human race but in the very largely positive response of the scientific community. Only the 'contrarians' are left behind. Rejecting old antagonisms, Pope Francis has elected to embrace science, reminding us none the less that the ethical questions raised by the debate cannot be resolved by science alone. Finding solutions is therefore an inter-disciplinary endeavour.

As the authors of this symposium recognise, social scientists must do their bit. This means, taking religion seriously as a full partner in the conversation. The challenge, however, is considerable and is best captured in a question. Is it possible for a set of disciplines, underpinned as they are by self-consciously secular philosophies of science, to engage with an area of human living that, almost by definition, contests this way of thinking?

It is at this point that the narrative in this chapter echoes the concluding section of the last. Both speak to the unexpectedness of the current agenda for mainstream social science. In many ways this is unsurprising given the roots of these disciplines in post-Enlightenment France: an intellectual milieu that saw rationality and empirical observation as the ultimate source of knowledge – a way of thinking that was formative in much of modern Europe. Europe, however, is increasingly seen as an 'exceptional' case in global terms, in the sense that its secularity is markedly more developed than in other global regions.[12] It follows that social-scientific tool kits – honed disproportionately in the atypical case – require significant reworking for 21st century use.

[1] The text of the encyclical is available at *w2.vatican.va/content/francesco/en/ encyclicals/documents/papa-francesco_20150524_enciclica-laudato-si.html*

[2] See *www.ipsp.org* for more information regarding the background and working of the IPSP. Contributing authors are listed, chapter by chapter.

[3] Both versions will be published by Cambridge University Press.

[4] Todd Johnson, Brian Grim and Gina Zurlo (eds), *World Religion Database* (Brill, 2016).

[5] Lori Beaman addresses this point in *Deep Equality in an Era of Religious Diversity* (Oxford University Press, 2017). She asks the following question: what might we discover if we turned our attention to the success stories of diverse living rather than dwelling disproportionately on points of conflict?

[6] See *thelancet.com/series/faith-based-health-care*

[7] This sentence is taken from the abstract to our chapter.

[8] For the text of the encyclical, see note 1.

[9] See *www.theguardian.com/commentisfree/2015/jun/18/guardian-view-on-laudato-si-pope-francis-cultural-revolution*

[10] 'Hope from the Pope', Editorial. *Nature*, 522 (7557), June 2015. Available at: *www.nature.com/news/hope-from-the-pope-1.17824*

[11] The articles were published in *Nature Climate Change*, 5 (10), September 2015. They are available at: *www.researchgate.net/publication/282175813_The_Pope%27s_fateful_vision_of_hope_for_society_and_the_planet*

[12] Grace Davie, *Europe: The Exceptional Case. Parameters of Faith in the Modern World* (Darton, Longman and Todd, 2002).

5
In conclusion

A set of cross-cutting themes runs through this essay. These themes were set out in the Introduction and include the following: the sustainability (or otherwise) of local churches, new (not always anticipated) opportunities, the turn to religion at every level of society, the notion of exceptional cases, and the need for innovative thinking in the social sciences. The following paragraphs revisit these questions, taking them – more or less – in reverse order.

The need for innovation in the social sciences is already clear. If your paradigms fail to predict – or even come close to predicting – the key events of the modern world (as these were presented at the end of Chapter 3) it is hard to argue that these models are fit for purpose. The reasons why were elaborated in Chapter 4 and concern, amongst other things, exceptionality. Approaches to religion developed in Europe (and to an extent in the US as well) lead to narrow and overly institutional definitions of religion. They also mask the complex realities of religion which play out on the global stage. This is not a story of secularisation.

The situation in London recalls the question of exceptionality in a different way. Is London an exceptional, or at least a distinctive, case in terms of the upturns in the religious statistics discovered in the city, or might this pattern be repeated elsewhere – in, for example, other parts of the UK influenced by migration? Or might London revert to the norm, and sooner rather than later? It isn't easy to say. The current situation is best understood in terms of a global narrative overlaying a European one – i.e. the six factors outlined in the Introduction to this report. As to the relative strengths of these two 'stories', only time will tell, but one point stands out. In global terms there is absolutely no incompatibility between being urban and being religious. The nature and forms of religiousness may well evolve but religion as such is as likely to flourish in the city as it is elsewhere.[1]

London, however, has other claims to distinctiveness, not least in the voting patterns revealed in the UK European Union membership referendum held on 23 June 2016. Overall, the British people voted by a narrow majority to leave the European Union – a result which defied predictions. The proportions of the vote varied, however, revealing markedly different patterns in different parts of the UK.[2] The proportion of 'Remainers' was highest in London, in Scotland and in Northern Ireland. Clearly different factors were at play in each of the three cases, but – paradoxically – all three were relatively relaxed about immigration (a dominant factor in the 'leave' vote). The reasoning, however, was various. In Scotland and Northern Ireland, immigration was a side-issue, each having comparatively low numbers of migrants. In these parts of the UK, moreover, it is emigration rather than immigration that has informed the recent – or relatively recent – past. In London, the explanation is different and resides largely in the presence of migrants themselves. On the one hand, their own votes counted, and on the other they were simply part of life. The taken-for-grantedness of migration in the capital is very different from the anticipatory fears that loomed large in middle England. The manifest welcome to Sadiq Khan, the Mayor of London, at his signing-in in Southwark Cathedral, provides a striking illustration of a religiously diverse city at ease with itself.

Approaches to religion developed in Europe lead to narrow and overly institutional definitions of religion.

A poll taken on the day of the Referendum tells us more about the religious vote in the country as a whole.[3] There were of course multiple factors at play: age, gender, ethnicity, class, income, education and so on, but in terms of religion, the key facts are the following: nearly six in ten (58%) of those describing themselves as Christian voted to leave, whereas seven in ten Muslims voted to remain. More detailed work on the voting *intentions* of different religious groups can be found in data drawn from the 2015 British Election Study.[4]

Siobhan McAndrew has analysed this material and observes a noticeable difference in voting intentions between Anglicans and the members of other religious groups, including some Christians. Catholics, for example, are more open to Europe than Anglicans. The relative reluctance of Anglicans to embrace a more cosmopolitan outlook suggests an elision – conscious or not – between Anglican attachment (both active and passive) and English (rather than British) identity,[5] a point to ponder in a year that marks the 500th anniversary of the Reformation.

> **The nature and forms of religiousness may well evolve but religion as such is as likely to flourish in the city as it is elsewhere.**

Such connections call to mind two related episodes. The first is European and reveals the tensions within the Catholic Church as it reacted to the escalating numbers of refugees arriving in Europe in the late summer of 2015. Pope Francis's reaction was to encourage European Catholics to make such people welcome, setting a high-profile example in accommodating refugee families in the Vatican. Rather different was the response of the Hungarian Bishop Laszlo Kiss-Rigo, who called on 'Christian' Europe to defend itself against a burgeoning flow of predominantly Muslim migrants.[6] It is all too easy to make judgements about who was right and who was wrong in this respect. There are, however, contextual as well as moral factors at play: Hungarians – we should recall – lived under the threat of Ottoman domination for centuries. In no way does this justify arbitrary exclusions; it does, however, help us to understand them.

The second episode is American, where once again the unimaginable happened in November 2016 when Donald Trump was elected President of the US, albeit falling short on the popular vote. A full compare and contrast between Brexit and Trump goes beyond the limits of a short conclusion but they undoubtedly raise similar issues. Both results were unexpected; both confounded the opinions of experts (the villains of the piece); both provoked consternation; and both saw significant elements of the 'religious' vote leaning in the same (pro-Brexit or pro-Trump) direction. Unsurprisingly, their more progressive co-religionists disagreed.

Quite apart from this, President Trump's initial and somewhat arbitrary actions concerning immigrants run counter to the thinking that emerged from our IPSP chapter. For example, generalising from the behaviour of extreme groups (that undoubtedly exist) to faith communities as a whole, in order to over-regulate the religious field, or suppress particular religions, is not what we were minded to recommend. Much more constructive – we argued – are policies that encourage religious diversity and affirm the capacity of well-intentioned groups to live well together. For the most part the United States has a proud history in this respect.

Reciprocal discourses

In response to a pervasive 'turn to religion' both within and beyond British society, I have argued not only for greater attention to the religious factor in current debate, but for a more sensitive discourse – more accurately set of discourses – with which to address this. There are, however, concomitant responsibilities. Calls that policy makers should be religiously literate and take note of religious sensibilities should be reciprocated. Those with religious interests, whether professional or academic, must themselves learn to be 'policy literate' if their ambitions are to be translated into effective action. This is a two-way learning process, insufficiently understood on both sides of the equation. Done well it fosters the partnerships already endorsed; done badly it dissipates – indeed squanders – much-needed potential.

> **Calls that policy makers should be religiously literate and take note of religious sensibilities should be reciprocated.**

Manifestly, *Laudato si'* got it right. It spoke powerfully to global elites, but in a language that resonated at every level of society: local, national and international. One example will suffice. It is taken from Chapter 4 of the encyclical entitled "Integral Ecology", in which the key concept is closely interrogated in its social and cultural as well as its economic and environmental forms:

> *Ecology, then, also involves protecting the cultural treasures of humanity in the broadest sense. More specifically, it calls for greater attention to local cultures when studying environmental problems, favouring a dialogue between scientific-technical language and the language of the people. Culture is more than*

what we have inherited from the past; it is also, and above all, a
living, dynamic and participatory present reality, which cannot
be excluded as we rethink the relationship between human
beings and the environment. (§143)

The sustainability of local churches (the point of departure for this essay), and their counterparts in other faiths, is central to this endeavour.

[1] See David Garbin and Anna Strhan (eds), *Religion and the Global City* (Bloomsbury, 2017).

[2] See the electoral maps available at *www.bbc.co.uk/news/uk-politics-36616028*

[3] See *lordashcroftpolls.com/2016/06/how-the-united-kingdom-voted-and-why/*

[4] See *blogs.lse.ac.uk/religionpublicsphere/2016/07/the-eu-referendum-religion-and-identity-analysing-the-british-election-study/*. See also *www.brin.ac.uk/2016/counting-religion-in-britain-june-2016/* and *www.brin.ac.uk/2017/how-religious-groups-voted-at-the-2016-referendum-on-britains-eu-membership*

[5] For more information on this elision see Abby Day's discussion of ethnic belonging in *Believing in Belonging: Belief and Social Identity in the Modern World* (OUP, 2013), pp 182-88. For ethnic belongers, migration is likely to threaten rather than renew the Christian heritage of this country.

[6] See for example the account in *www.washingtonpost.com/world/hungarian-bishop-says-pope-is-wrong-about-refugees/2015/09/07/fcba72e6-558a-11e5-9f54-1ea23f6e02f3_story.html*